1 MONTH OF
FREE
READING

at
www.ForgottenBooks.com

By purchasing this book you are eligible for one month membership to ForgottenBooks.com, giving you unlimited access to our entire collection of over 1,000,000 titles via our web site and mobile apps.

To claim your free month visit:

www.forgottenbooks.com/free789808

ISBN 978-0-484-42581-0
PIBN 10789808

CHRIST HIS OWN INTERPRETER

AND

OTHER SERMONS

BY

J. E. RANKIN

BOSTON

D. LOTHROP & CO., FRANKLIN ST.

NEW YORK

H. E. SIMMONS, 150 NASSAU ST.

TABLE OF CONTENTS.

	PAGE
CHRIST HIS OWN INTERPRETER	1
HOLDING FAST THE FORM OF SOUND WORDS.	21
THE RACE SOLVENT	39
LIFE ETERNAL.	59
THE SENSE OF PROPERTY IN SIN	77

JOHN X: 11—"I am the good Shepherd: the good Shepherd giveth his life for the sheep."

If there ever was a Being, wearing the human form and living among men, who knew Himself and why He came here it was the Man Christ Jesus. He always walked in the shadow of the Cross: He never forgot that He came here to do the Father's will. Self-knowledge is the most difficult knowledge which men ever attain. There is no sphynx in Egypt like the sphynx in a man's bosom. Men think too much or too little of themselves. They pride themselves on being what they are not: on having a sphere which is not theirs. They undertake to do what they can not do : they leave undone what they might do. All from want of self-knowledge.

How many a man dies, feeling that his life has been a failure; that he has not taken it by the right handle; that somehow he has missed the tide that, taken at its flood, would have borne him on to fortune; and therefore his shallows and his miseries. For one man, who knows why he is here, and what God has for him to do;

who adjusts himself to his surroundings; who fits into things as a horse into his harness, and works there, and who feels that whatever work other men have, this is his work from God, this is why God sent him into the world; there are hundreds of men to whom life is a joke, of which they seem to be the butt; is a conundrum which they are trying to guess; a problem which they are trying to solve; a mystery which they are trying to penetrate.

You and I, as we look back four hundred years, and see Martin Luther, that moral Hercules, trying to let in the River of Life upon those Augean stables at Rome, where had gathered the moral filth of centuries; nailing the truth to the church door at Wittenberg; burning the Pope's bull publicly before the city's gates; putting the Word of God into the German vernacular, so that David and Isaiah, John and Paul could, in his terse phrase, speak Dutch; you and I know why Martin Luther was born, and for what cause he came into the world. In a good measure he knew it himself; but not as we do; not as God did. For, in some sense, the vantage-ground which history gives us, if we find God in it, is like the vantage-ground which He has, to whom time is one eternal now; who knows the end from the beginning; who sees the plant in the seed; the oak in the acorn; the man in the boy; His ministers that do His pleasure in men whose breath is in their nostrils. God only can interpret a man to himself; can interpret a man to his fellows.

The subject which I want to discuss this morning is this :

CHRIST, HIS OWN INTERPRETER.

" I am the good Shepherd ; the good Shepherd giveth His life for the sheep."

I. The interpretations which have been put upon Christ's person and work are very various. These have been largely determined by the standpoint from which men have looked at Him. What is the testimony of His contemporaries? Men who knew Him in His life ; men who companied with Him, who heard His words and saw His works ; men who were born of His Spirit immediately after His death ; nay for three centuries after His death ; put their interpretation into one single word : worship ! They never doubted that He was God ! Three centuries of worship ! This is the first step in the Christology of the Church. Then and not till then Arianism. They had an experience of His power to forgive sin ; of His power to transform their fallen nature, such that they could say nothing less than those words of Peter : " Thou art the Son of the living God ;" those words of Thomas : " My Lord and my God !" There was such an inscrutable mystery about Him ; He had such sovereignty relating to the powers of nature ; to disease, as its healer ; to sorrow and to sin, as a fellow-sufferer ; to the elements, as their master and Lord ; even to death itself, that they could put no other interpretation upon Him. What manner of Man is this ! They knew He was more than man !

We are nearly nineteen centuries from the commence-
ment of the Christian era.. In that period Christian experience has not changed its nature. That which convinced the woman of Samaria; that which convinced
Andrew and Peter; that which convinced John and Paul
of the divinity of Christ; that He came here to be a
propitiation for the sins of the world; that which in-
duced them to repent and believe in Him has not changed.
There are no new tests to be applied to these things. It is
interesting for the student of ecclesiastical history to read
about Arianism, the theory that Christ was superhuman
without being divine; about Patripassianism, the theory
that He was the one God dwelling in a human body;
the Father, before the incarnation, the Son, afterward;
about Nestorianism, the theory which gives us in Him
both man and God, distinct from each other, but no
God-Man. But it is a great deal more interesting to me
to know that for three centuries, the Christian Church,
without undertaking to define just what she believed as
to the mode of His being, accepted this Jesus of Nazareth as a Being to be worshipped.

What we want in history is to know just how a histor-
cal character impressed Himself upon His contemporaries.
We want to put ourselves in their place and see out of
their eyes. We want the power, not to reconstruct Him
out of the materials in our hands, real or imaginary; not
to argue that He must have been this or that to make out
our hypothesis; but to reproduce Him from the impres-
sions He made; from the estimates made of Him by His
contemporaries; to set Him again amid the surroundings

of His time, and find out what men thought of Him then. That is the Man we want to know. For three centuries Christ was worshipped. This is just contrary to the mythical theory of accounting for what was wonderful in His career; as if things, not in themselves supernatural, should in the course of centuries come to be so regarded; as moss gathers on stones.

The Christian era opens. The world begins to count its age anew. Some Being has lived and died, who, for three hundred years, by them who knew Him best and loved Him most, is worshipped as God. There is no mythical character of divinity that can gather upon such a character as this. All the literature about Christ that has ever been produced ; and the last generation has been the most prolific of all ; cannot help us to the understanding of such a character, as do the simple annals of the Gospel.

What is the testimony of prophecy ? It is a wonderful fact that to-day, when the angry seas of all kinds of criticism are dashing against the Word of God, there is nothing that so keeps it from going to pieces as the Man Christ Jesus. He is its Alpha and Omega. It is as though the roots of the Tree of Life had so gone into the soil of the Bible that they hold this soil together. If you say, that previous to the history of Joseph the sacred narrative is rather a compilation of traditions than any connected history, as is the language of what is called the higher criticism of to-day, I point you to these words in the third chapter of Genesis: "It shall bruise thy head, and thou shall bruise his heel." Here is a line of prophetic light that must have been written by the finger of God.   Here is the beginning of all prophecy relative to the Son of Man ; the first hint of Bethlehem and Calvary. Here is something that differentiates the narrative of the first things in Genesis, from the traditions of other nations which seem to be parallel with it.   It has the Man Christ Jesus in it ; it has in it the purpose of God to become incarnate.   And from this beginning, there, among those dim Eden highlands, this stream of prophecy flows through the whole book until it is lost in that great sea of life, in The Revelation.   This is the seed of Abraham, in whom all the nations of the earth shall be blessed; the seed of David, of whom the Lord swore in truth, " Of the fruit of thy body will I set upon thy throne;" the One of whom Isaiah speaks, " Behold a virgin shall conceive and bear a Son, and thou shalt call His name Immanuel;" and Daniel, where he says, " And after three score and two weeks shall Messiah be cut off, but not for Himself."

There are two things respecting the Old Testament which never can be overthrown :   The fact that its burden of history, type, prophecy, is the Man Christ Jesus, and the other fact that to its genuineness and authority as well as to the character of its contents, He Himself has given this testimony : " Search the Scriptures, for in them ye think ye have eternal life ; and they are they which testify of me."   These are Christ's witnesses, to which He appealed on that wonderful walk to Emmaus. And beginning at Moses and all the prophets He expounded unto them in all the Scriptures the thing concerning Himself. He found things concerning Himself in Moses, in David, in Isaiah, in Jeremiah, in Ezekiel, in Daniel, in Micah, in Zechariah, in Malachi. And these things are there to-day with His divine indorsement. And these things are what hold the Bible together. For He believed them to relate to Himself. And the book, which for centuries before His advent contained them, must be a book from God.

II. The interpretation put upon Christ is said to be different, in different sacred writers, according to their temperament and mental structure.

There is a great deal said about the Pauline theology as something distinct from that of John, from that of Christ, Paul's Master and Lord. There are those who do not regard John or the Saviour as ever teaching the doctrine of a vicarious atonement; of ever conceiving that it was Christ's commission from the Father to make, nay to become a propitiation for the sins of the whole world. They say the Apostle Paul foisted this dogma into Christian theology. It is true, that the Christology of the Gospels, of the Evangelists, is like the science of material things in nature. It is not systematized. The Gospels are only Memorabilia ; like Xenophon's Memorabilia of Socrates. Facts are given without classification. For, both in things material and things spiritual, facts are the things with which men have the most to do. Christology is only the science of Christ's nature and work as gathered from the facts recorded in His life. The function of the Apostle Paul, more especially in the Epistle to the Romans, was like that of Linnaeus in

Botany: to take these facts and derive from them a principle, a law, a doctrine; to arrange them in their proper
order; to articulate the body of Christian doctrine,
gathering up and bringing together different members
scattered through Christ's own life, teachings and work.

I claim not only that there is no antagonism between
the theology of St. John and that of St. Paul, but that
St. Paul is the best exponent of St. John's theology, better
even than St. John himself. You cannot find a statement
of St. John's theology better than this: " I am crucified
with Christ; nevertheless, I live, yet not I, but Christ
liveth in me." There is an experimental theology, a
mystical theology; a theology derived from the side of
the spirit, from the side of experience, which is just as
genuine as the theology of the intellect, but no more so.
The disciple that leaned in the Master's bosom and was
privileged to ask Him hard questions, affected this
theology. His nature was gentle, his conceptions of
the truth spiritual and experimental, rather than intellectual and logical. We are told in these days that " the
doctrines that men regarded as parts of orthodoxy are
the reflections of the social condition in which they
were formulated," the voice of the new theology; that
St. Paul so conceived of, the economy of grace because of
the peculiarities of Roman society and Roman authority;
and that now, since Rome is no more, and Roman heathenism is no more, the power of the Gospel has changed
all this, and so good-bye to the old ideas of God's sovereignty, man's depravity. This is the attitude of what
is called the new theology, the new movement. This

statement implies a very loose conception of what inspiration is in the way of guarding the sacred writers from mistaking what in Christianity is permanent from what is temporary. The Pauline aspects of truth then are not in the nature of things, but were in the political economy of ancient Rome, and so the apostle, who was writing only for a single generation and not for all time, is left to foist materials into his Epistles which might help the Christians at Rome, but which are a hindrance to Christians in America, who are now trying to work themselves free of them under the leadership of these new theologians, these modern mystics, who are navigating new seas, expecting new continents.

I have no doubt of the debt which humanity owes to the jurisprudence of the Romans. It is the best formulation of the reign of law in civil affairs up to that time ever made. It has doubtless had its bearing upon everything governmental that has come after it. We are debtors to it every day we live. But the idea of law was just as really in Nature, in Judaism, as in Roman jurisprudence; and what need to look to imperial Rome to discover the idea of God's sovereignty? And where in imperial Rome was the idea of vicarious atonement as the Jews had it? The Mosaic system had these things as ancient Rome never had them. This, humanly speaking, is what Mosaism was for. And if it is true, as Jesus says it is, that He came not to destroy the law and the prophets, but to fulfill them, where but in Judaism are we to look for the pre-intimations of His kingdom? Judaism, like Paganism in Rome, passes away.

But, what in Judaism was typical and symbolical of the Kingdom of the Lord Jesus Christ, abideth forever. Read the Epistle to the Hebrews, and see how the Old Dispensation unfolds into the New, as à bud unfolds into the flower.

That man has read the theology of St. Paul in vain, who finds in it only a system of dry bones, like the bones of a skeleton; a system of salvation by substitution; legal and judicial. I want to quote here from a Unitarian, who will not be partial on this question. I refer to Athanase Coquerel, the younger, in his "First Historical Transformations of Christianity." This is what he says: "The whole theology of Paul rests not only upon the antagonism of Christianity, which he calls faith, with Mosaism, which he calls law; but upon the more radical opposition of the Jewish principle to the Christian principle; of exterior and formalistic legality to the interior life of the spirit. All ceremonial religions, all external rules, all rituals, all codes, are powerless to sanctify, because they bear upon the outer life of the human being. It is by the spirit alone, by the heart, the conscience, the real feelings, the inner life, that man becomes holy and just, because it is by these alone that man subjects to the influence of truth and love the rest of all his faculties; the source whence all his actions spring. Faith, according to Paul, does not reduce itself merely to the fact that one does not doubt such or such a doctrine; it is the adhesion of the entire soul, convinced, penetrated, regenerated, embracing with all its strength, truth, Christ, God. If Paul be inquired of,

how Jesus saves souls, there are two responses, which he
gives by turn.   In truth, he entertained two theories of
salvation, one mystic and emotional, the other dogmatic
and argumentative.   He often gives one alone of these
as sufficient ; and two inverse series of passages might be
arranged, wherein each would seem to be all, while the
other is passed over in silence.   The mystical theory is
that of the union of the believer with Him in whom he
believes.   Christ is wholly united to God, and he who believes in God through Christ is united closely to Christ,
and through Christ to God.   This idea, which is found
again in St. John, and which emanates directly from
Christ Himself, is carried very far by our apostle.   The
Christian is to live the life of His Master ; to die and
rise again ; that is, associate Himself with the crises
which He has passed through, and come forth from them
triumphant.''
The mystical theory is something which is not addressed to the head ; it cannot be proved by argument.
It is intuitional.   It proves itself as a flash of light
beaming upon the darkness.   Hear one of its affirma-
tions : " We know that we have passed from death unto
life !''   Wonderful transition !   How do we know ?   Because we are justified by faith ?   This is not the method
under consideration.   " We know that we have passed
from death unto life, because we love the brethren !''   It
is a shorter cut than that though didactic theology.   But
the conclusion is the same.   " Ye have an unction from
the Holy One, and ye know all things.''   This mystical
theology is that which protects the great body of

Christians from the attacks made upon their faith. But, after all, the standards of faith are to be formulated only by the head. It will not do to underrate the other theology of St. Paul. Theology, as a science, never can be anything but a philosophy derived from great universal facts; facts logically arranged, not by the heart, but by the head. Christian experience verifies it, but never formulates it. If the mystics formulate theological truth, they go into all sorts of extravagances. Christian experience is but the annals of the Gospels over again, only in the realm of the spirit; the blind receiving their sight, the deaf hearing, the dead raised to life. It all crystallizes in obedience to the same law. When I want to study into the philosophy of God's economy; to come at the balance of the great magnitudes, which make their serene march in the firmament of His love; to see how God can be just and yet justify him that believeth, I ask for the guidance of St. Paul; I ask for him whose flight of thought is like that of an eagle, and whose wing never tires. When I want to get at the heart of the Gospel; to know the fact about God's love, while I let the philosophy go, to behold the Lamb of God, that taketh away the sin of the world, I ask for the guidance of St. John. In the one I find theology as a science; in the other theology as an experience.

III. But what is the Christology of Christ? How does He speak of Himself? As already intimated, if any Being bearing the human form ever knew Himself, knew His mission upon the earth, it was this Jesus of Nazareth. He walked in the light of the Father's love. He always had this testimony, that He pleased God. What does He mean, when He says in the text, "I am the good shepherd; the good shepherd giveth his life for the sheep?" Is it not the same as when he said, "And I, if I be lifted up, will draw all men unto me?"

He conceives, in the first place, of mankind as lost; as wandering over this planet, generation after generation, like unshepherded sheep in a wilderness; having no hope, and without God, in the world. He comes here, not in the form of some angelic messenger, lighting down from Heaven, and speaking to them from a higher plane. For His work His true humanity is just as needful as His divinity. He comes here, born of a woman; taking the fashion of this race of lost ones, God's alienated ones; He, who in Heaven thought it not robbery to be equal with God; with whom the Father was well pleased. He comes here in poverty, so that He can have a fellow-feeling for the poor. He keeps company with publicans and sinners, so that he is called their friend. He heals their sicknesses. He preaches to them the good news of forgiveness. What is his aim in all this? It is to gather them back to the Father's fold; to establish the Kingdom of God among men. Does He succeed? He lives between three and four years as a public teacher; speaks as never man spake; performs wonders, such as never man performed; appeals to the Sacred Book of His own countrymen to substantiate His claims to be their Messiah. With what result? Now I want those who believe that Jesus Christ came here merely as

a teacher, to look at this fact, that, while the testimony
of the ages is that He is, what He never called Himself,.
the Great Teacher; while all other human teachers pale
before him their ineffectual fires; when He died, He
had gathered around Himself twelve disciples and a few
women, and the Jewish populace cried, " Not this man,
but Barabbas!   Away with Him! crucify Him! crucify
Him!"   He, whose dominion was to be from sea to sea,
and from the river unto the ends of the earth!   Doubtless, the grandest factor of His errand here had not yet
been reached.

Mark this : In the text this Jesus of Nazareth does not
conceive of Himself merely as a shepherd.   Up to the
time of His death He had not begun to draw all men to
Himself.   He conceives of Himself as a shepherd who
proposes to put Himself between this flock of lost ones
and death ; this great human march of the generations
and eternal ruin.   " The good shepherd giveth His life
for the sheep."   The first function of the shepherd is
to feed the flock.   But the shepherd has another function,
that of protection; that of deliverance.   You remember
what the stripling David said in the presence of King Saul:
" Thy servant kept his father's sheep, and there came a
lion and a bear and took a lamb out of the flock, and I
went out after him and smote him and delivered it out
of his mouth, and when he arose against me I caught
him by his beard, and smote him and slew him."   Thy
servant slew both the lion and the bear.   And Dr.
Thomson, in his " Land and the Book," says he has
known more than one case where the faithful shepherd

has died in defense of his flock from the attacks of wild beasts, and he mentions one man who was actually hacked to pieces by three Bedouin robbers and died among the sheep he was defending.   Now read again the words of the context: " I am the good shepherd and know my sheep, and am known of mine.   And I lay down my life for the sheep."

The greatest difficulty which the human mind discovers in the economy of God is this : That he has created a race of beings to whom such a struggle as we read of in all the ages, as we witness, is incident ; and yet holds Himself aloof from it ; does nothing to mitigate its severity, or to afford us relief.   You say : "This vicarious nature of the Atonement is a figment of theologians ; is unreasonable."   I tell you that its first function is precisely here ; to prove that the Creator is not a cold and distant spectator of this struggle ; that He is in it Himself ; that He has pitted Himself as man's champion against sin.   One of the greatest mysteries of the Godhead, the Incarnation ; another of its greatest mysteries, the Atonement ; life in human flesh and blood, death in human flesh and blood ; is for this very purpose : to show how God stands with reference to evil in humanity ; with reference to sin and to sinners.   God is not tarrying to see how we shall come out of this struggle. In Christ Jesus, His Son, He is involved in this struggle with us.

Dr. Channing thinks Unitarianism better than Orthodoxy, because it gives man a more agreeable idea of God's moral government.   " He lives," he says, "in the midst

of a glorious universe which was meant to be a witness
and preacher of the Divinity.'' The thing wanted is a
truthful idea of God's government. Is there no voice of
sadness arising amid this glorious universe? Is there no
deep undertone of discord breaking in upon nature's
hymn of praise? And if there is, has it never gone up to the
ear of God? And is God indifferent to it? And if
not, how does He express Himself? We remember Mrs.
Browning's '' Cry of the Human '':

'' There is no God," the foolish saith; but none, there is no sorrow,
And nature oft the cry of faith in bitter need will borrow.
Eyes which the preacher could not school by wayside graves are raised,
And lips say God be pitiful! who ne'er said, God be praised.

The battle hurtles on the plains, earth feels new scythes upon her,
We reap our brothers for the wrains, and call the harvest honor!
Draw face to face, front line to line, one image all inherit—
Then kill, curse on, by that same sign: clay, clay, and spirit, spirit.

We pray together at the kirk, for mercy, mercy, solely, solely:
Hands weary with the evil work, we lift them to the Holy.
The corpse is calm upon our knee, its spirit bright before Thee;
Between them, worse than either, we: without the rest of glory.

We sit on hills our childhood wist, woods, hamlets, streams beholding:
The sun strikes through the farthest mist, the city's spire to golden,
The city's golden spire, it was, when hope and health were strongest;
But, but now it is the churchyard grass, we look upon the longest.

And soon all vision waxeth dull: men whisper, '' He is dying!''
We cry no more, '' Be pitiful!'' we have no strength for crying:
No strength, no need. Then, soul of mine, look up and triumph
        rather:
Lo in the depth of God's Divine, the Son abjures the Father!

Only the Son of Man utters the full human cry, " My
God, My God, why hast thou forsaken me ? "

There is no sensitive soul, that looks at life as it is,
which is not filled with unutterable sadness ; heathenism
abroad, heathenism at our very doors, heathenism in our
souls. And, I think, the more a man has the likeness of
God, the more sadness he must have. Now, if in our
theology, whether it be that of the head or the heart, for
I believe they are one in the true believer, we have a
place for God in Christ ; for God in the Man of sorrows,
and acquainted with grief; if God in His infinite fatherhood, if Christ in his infinite brotherhood is there ; I do
not say the mystery of God's government is all solved,
but I say it is greatly relieved. I say, if in our theology
God is in Christ reconciling the world unto Himself, not
imputing their trespasses unto them, then He has not
left us alone !

I do not hold to the mere juridical theory of the
Atonement ; that is, that Christ was our substitute on the
cross, and now that God accepts us on purely forensic
grounds. This is anatomic theology ; true, but not all
the truth ; any more than the bones are all the body. I
believe that God accepts the believer in Christ Jesus ;
but the condition of this acceptance, on the believer's
side, is faith. And here comes in the experimental, the
mystical theology, which is no more all of theology than
flesh and blood are all of the body. Nor would the mere
juridical view be in harmony with the context. It is not
enough for the Good Shepherd to give His life for the
sheep. Here is where the most valiant of earthly shep-

herds fails of being a type of Christ.   The earthly shepherd falls amid his sheep about to die, for after his death
who can protect them?   But how about the Good Shepherd?   The Good Shepherd lays down his life that He
may take it again; and that he may awaken it in the
lost, unsheperded ones for whom He dies.   And not until
He has risen again and ascended to His Father and the
Holy Spirit, the Comforter, has been shed forth does
even His perfect work move the hearts of men.   It is
only then it is interpreted to them.

   The Christology, the science of Christ, we hold is
worthless unless it move us to a Christ-like life ; that is,
a life along His line of work, a life whose upward carri-
age springs from love to God and the desire to please
Him; if we do not put ourselves under humanity to com-
fort, to raise, to serve it even as He did.   If Christ died
for us, and we believe it and feel it, it is the main-spring
of all our living!   The Christian morality of this generation of Christians has sprung from just this source.   I
mean parents believing this have trained up those who
are now men and women from the belief in a vicarious
atonement.   This is St. Paul's interpretation of the bearing of this work of Christ upon our lives.   Christ in our
stead then ; we in Christ's stead now.   "And that He
died for all, that they which live should henceforth not
live unto themselves, but unto Him who died for them."
St. John has the same inference : "Hereby perceive we
the love of God for us, because He laid down His life
for us; and we ought to lay down our lives for the
brethren."   The height a stream of water will rise, de-

pends upon the head it has among the hills. The height
of our Christian morality is to be determined in the
same way. If it have its head in loving God, because
He has first loved us, if it spring from love to God incarnate for our sakes, love to God in Christ, reconciling
the world unto Himself, that is one kind of morality.
It makes heroes and heroines. It makes martyrs. If we
accept the Good Shepherd as laying down His life for
us; if in our lives we are baptized into His sacrificial
death, then we have a right to claim freedom from the
consequences of sin through Him Then is it true that
we have beheld the Lamb of God which taketh away the
sin of the world.

I've seen the Good Shepherd in the hands of His foes,
His back was sore smitten from their pitiless blows;
His brow was encircled with the thorns pressed above,
But, ah! it was kingly and so radiant with love.

O Shepherd, Good Shepherd! there thus nailed to the tree,
Thy hands they have wounded, and Thy side, too, I see;
Thy face has strange pallor, and how labored Thy breath,
Thou'rt walking the Valley of the Shadow of Death.

O Shepherd, Good Shepherd! my poor name write it now,
In blood that down trickles from Thy feet and Thy brow;
And there where they've wounded with the spear-thrust Thy side.
They've cloven a refuge where a sinner may bide.

O Shepherd, Good Shepherd! Thou art gone up on high,
Art seated in glory in Thy own native sky;
The love that once ransomed is a love that will keep,
Good Shepherd, that gavest thus Thy life for the sheep,

II

HOLDING FAST THE FORM OF SOUND WORDS.

2 TIM. 1, 13 : "Hold fast the form of sound words, which thou hast heard from me in faith and love, which is in Christ Jesus."

Every fresh generation comes upon the stage, saying to the world, "Behold, I make all things new." And in a certain sense this is true. Every new generation fashions its own habiliments of thought and of life. Spring creeps upon winter with the same prophecy; seems to herself to have changed the whole framework of things, because she has clothed them anew; because she is the dress-maker among the seasons. She does not remember that all her freshness and beauty, whether of tree, vegetable, or grass, is rooted and nourished in the old; and that the very bones of the earth, her minerals, are all the time contributing to the earth's graces. The soil, which is not indebted to the rocks, is barren ; has nothing to give forth in verdure.

The newness, which passes upon the new generation, of humanity's thought, comes out of the old earth, the everlasting hills ; just as it is in nature. The fathers, where are they ? And the prophets, do they live forever ?

The fathers are in their children, and the prophets do live in the fulfillment of their predictions. The literature of the Bible is quite as much alive among men as its theology and its ethics. Young men sometimes discuss the question, "What is originality?" It is a pretty conclusive way to answer this question to say, what every thinking man knows, that beyond the works of a limited number of great minds, naturally or supernaturally inspired, he needs very few books. A few books contain it all. The world of thought, like the material world, hides her richness in the hills. And the verdure of each fresh generation of thought is fed from those hidden resources; is spread thinly over the surface, like the grass and the trees. All new writers of any freshness bring forth new aspects, new relations of old truth. For all truth is old; as old as God. And like love, which it is, it has its seat in the bosom of God.

This is no less true of theology than anything else. Each new generation comes, saying of old beliefs: "Behold I make all things new!" But, so far as what is presented is true, it is old truth in a new light; and so far as it is not true, it is old error in a new light. This generation has as yet said nothing on eschatology which has not been said—I will not say better said—centuries ago. The fathers of the early centuries seem to have had about the same degree of illumination as has fallen to our lot, even in this nineteenth century of the Christian era.

The subject which I shall this morning discuss is

THE DUTY OF HOLDING FAST THE FORM OF SOUND WORDS.

I. I remark that no thought is definite, so that it can be looked at and circumscribed, until it has been put into language. It must have landmarks to show that it has been taken up. The very word definite implies that a thought has been thus defined; limited, as by measurement, by actual survey; fenced in, as by a boundary, from something else which does not belong to it; fenced out from something to which it does not belong. There is nothing that shows a man how little he knows, and how imperfectly he knows it, like getting him to write it down. Two disputants, who believe their views are world-wide apart, and who can tilt at each for hours, in unwritten speech, disagreeing only in definitions, come to pin them down to exact language, often find they think pretty much alike; discover they have been fighting men of straw. Indeed, there is no precise thought without precise language. No man has any precise thought in any earthly science until he has put it, or seen it put, into language. What we speak is breath. It goes forth into the air, and never can be gathered back again. It is more evanescent than water spilt on the ground. You may have been present when an effort has been made in some legislative body to have recorded the unfortunate utterance of some member who is charged with having violated the proprieties of the place. It is next to impossible to get his exact words. It is always impossible to repeat his intonations and inflexions. But what a man puts down in black and white, as we say;

what he writes down, he looks at as an entity, his own creation. Thought is spirit; language embodying that thought is spirit incarnate. The Jews wanted the Roman Governor to modify the inscription which he had put above the Cross. He replied: "What I have written, I have written." Many a man will make a bargain with you, which, if not put in writing, he will upon occasion violate. It has been urged that all marriage contracts ought to be put into writing. Why not? None are more important. Why should not a man be compelled to say in words, over his own signature, that which he so thoughtlessly and so insinuatingly suggests, by look, tone, gift; in a thousand nameless ways?

If all thought needs to be put into language in order to limit it, to make it definite and precise, this is especially true in religion. Religion has to do with what in its very nature is vague and indistinct, because it relates to the unseen world : because it relates to spirit instead of matter.

In his synthetic philosophy, Herbert Spencer has shown how difficult it is to form a distinct conception of some things with which we seem to be most familiar: the earth for example. "When on the seashore we note how the hulls of distant vessels are hidden below the horizon, and how of still remoter vessels only the uppermost sails are visible, we realize with tolerable clearness the slight curvature of that portion of the sea's surface which lies before us. But when we seek in imagination to follow out its curved surface as it actually exists, slowly bending

round until all its meridians, meet in a point eight thousand miles below our feet, we find ourselves utterly baf-
fled.   We cannot conceive, in its real form and magnitude, even that small segment of the globe which extends
a hundred miles on every side of us; much less of the
globe as a whole.   The piece of rock on which we stand
can be mentally represented with something like com-
pleteness. . We find ourselves able to think of its top,
its sides, and its under surfaces at the same time, or so
nearly at the same time that they seem all present in
consciousness together; and so we can form what we call
conception of the rock.   But to do the like of the earth
we find impossible.   Yet we habitually speak as though
we had an idea of the earth, as though we could think
of it as of minor objects.''

We say of the earth that it is round.   This gives our
thought definiteness. ' As taught in the school we conceive of it as like an apple or a ball; the ships of the
ocean like flies crawling around it.; although take it as
far as the eye or the telescope can reach, it has its hills
and mountains, its valleys and ocean depths, with an
average surface which we characterize as flat.   We judge
of the earth by what we have under our feet, under our
eye.' We judge of the animal and vegetable life upon it
by what we see around us. We judge of the people in
the same manner.   But when we come to conceive of it
as one great planet, with all its material varieties and
diversities ; with its millions of beings like ourselves ;
with its greater millions of inferior animals in earth, sea
and air ; with its fauna and flora, according to its lati-

tude; then we break down. It is not knowable. It is
not knowable to us by one act of cognition, or a great
many acts put together.

There are those who say that since our knowledge of
God is so indefinite and imperfect, since it is impossible
for us to conceive of Him as one whole, it is better that
we should not put our thoughts into language at all.
The argument is just as good when applied to the earth.
Our knowledge of the earth is indefinite and imperfect.
It is impossible for us to conceive of the earth as a whole.
The rotundity of the earth, made up of mountain heights
and ocean depths, seems almost an impossible thing.
The earth round, with mountains so high, with oceans
so deep! But we still keep speaking of it as round;
indeed we still keep proving it to be round, by sailing
around it. It is true there is not an attribute of God
that is knowable by mental cognition. We say He is a
spirit. But what is a spirit? We say He is infinite.
But what is infinite? We say He is eternal. But what
is eternity? We say He is unchangeable. But what is
unchangeableness? In the same sense that we know
nothing about the rotundity of the earth, so we know
nothing about God. We cannot conceive of one of His
attributes. But is that any reason why we should not
try to put our belief about Him, our thought about Him,
into words? The more difficult of apprehension a subject may be, the more important for us to try and get
some definite conception of thought about it. The reason why some religious denominations have no definite
belief is because they have never tried to put their belief

into words.   Words would have precipitated it, as rain
is precipitated by condensation ; would have crystallized
it, as water is crystallized by freezing.   Words would
show them what they do believe ; perhaps that they believe nothing.

A great deal has been said in this generation in dis-
paragement of creeds, as though creeds were a kind of
infernal machine, where the mind of man is racked
and his freedom impinged on by the Christian Churches.
But a creed is only the form of thought, the formulated
thinking, in any generation respecting God and the
things of God.   The creed-makers have been the great
benefactors of the race.   They have made the knowledge
of men definite.   They have challenged errors, that in
ghostly guise have gone stalking over the field of thought,
and made them down, while truth has taken their place.

II. No thought in theology is safe, can be kept, unless
it is put into words.   The science of God and of man
in his relation to God is condemnatory of man, is min-
atory toward him, as he is by nature.   Nothing is more
natural than that man should antagonize it.   It antago-
nizes him, as he is here in the world, as he lives, as he
dies.   If he can he will try to wrest it, as the direction
of light is wrested, bent from directness, by passing
through the medium of water.   He always will wrest it
unless he be put upon his guard.

The latest test to which the destructive criticism is
subjecting Revelation is what is called our ethical consciousness.   This means the inward law of morals, which
humanity· finds within itself; what it conceives to be

equitable and honorable as between man and God. If there is anything which purports to have come from God that conflicts with this ethical consciousness, or offends it, that the higher criticism rejects. There is nothing new in this position. It is the position which all rationalists take with regard to what is tested by pure reason. We say of things that God has revealed, that they do not accord with our reason, and therefore we will not receive them. This is rationalism. The Bible is to go up or down, according as it does or does not accord with our reason. When the missionaries told the Emperor of Siam that they came from a country where water became so solid that his royal elephants could walk on it, he replied that they had told him lies enough before, but this was the greatest lie of them all. He knew nothing about the law by which at a certain temperature water crystallizes into ice. But we have been familiar with such a law from our birth. Nearly all the wonders of modern civilization may well challenge the faith of the pagan nations; the movements of machinery by the power of steam; the transmission of thought on the wings of light; the hearing of the human voice hundreds of miles from the speaker! Tested by the reason of pagan nations, what more impossible? But the difference between the civilized and the barbarian is not like the difference between the infinite and the finite. There may be infinite laws, which are as much beyond the power of finite reason to grasp, to recognize, as the laws of modern discoveries are beyond the reason of the heathen. A thing may seem unrea-

sonable to us, only because it transcends our powers of
thought; it is in a sphere beyond any of our observation or experience. So much for rationalism.

Our ethical consciousness, as it is called, is the ethical
consciousness of a fallen race. And here we have not
merely the disability of being finite, as against God's
being infinite, but the greater disability of being sinful,
as against God's being holy. Our ethical standards are
unsafe because the ethics of our lives are the precise
sphere in which God's law bears upon us disagreeably.
God says "Thou shalt, and thou shalt not." There is a
homely proverb:

> "No man e'er felt the halter draw,
> With good opinion of the law."

The ethical consciousness of a rogue is not the ethical
consciousness of an honest man. Of the men under
conviction of crime to-day not one in a hundred feels
that he has been honestly tried and condemned. I never
talked much with a man under sentence of crime who
did not seem to find it difficult to keep from arguing
over and over again that he ought not to have been con-
victed. It was a monomania with him. The ethical
consciousness of the penitent thief was: "And we justly;
but this man hath done nothing amiss." A man who
sees his sins through the tearful eyes of a penitent, while
he gets glimpses of the rainbow of God's love, does not
forget that the ominous clouds against which this rainbow lies are big with the thunders of wrath, the penalties
of law; and that even this rainbow-form has been
abstracted from that blackness of darkness lately rup-

tured by a thunder-burst, and yielding up its contents, to bless his soul.

The ethical consciousness of man is good, so far as it goes; as to what we can trust it for. But it always depends upon whether he is an interested party. It was the custom of Socrates before answering a question put by a disciple to ask the questioner, what manner of man he was himself? No judge of any character would try a case where the decision was to affect himself, his name, his property. He would see that his ethical consciousness could not be relied on for this. God did not allow King David to sit·on his own case, as between himself and Uriah, the Hittite. He knew he could not be trusted. The man who could so maliciously plot such a wrong thing, and could so ignominiously hide it, needed to see his sin masquerade before him, under another's name before his ethical consciousness was fit to be trusted. There are sins as to which it is comparatively safe to trust a man's ethical consciousness. They are the sins which are committed by his neighbor, and especially by his neighbor against himself. The instinct of the ethical consciousness is immediate. It says, "The man that hath done this thing shall surely die."

The ethical consciousness is not an organ like the eye; or, rather like the eye, the ethical consciousness is not a cold and dead organ, to be looked through by somebody else. It is the man himself looking at great moral questions. What makes the eye of an opium-eater unreliable, is that he is an opium-eater, and the drug has impaired the correctness of his vision. A medical man would

say: "The perceptive cerebral centres are blunted."
It is not somebody else looking through his eye that sees
imperfectly, whose vision is impaired. It is himself.
The Bible says: "There is a way that seemeth right to
a man; but the end thereof are the ways of death."
Why should a way seem right when it is not right? This
is the sphere of man's ethical consciousness; can he not
trust it? And if it is unreliable once, may it not be unreliable again? Ah! the perceptive cerebral centres of
his soul are blunted. We speak of a chronometer, which
keeps perfect time; of a chronometer which has not lost
a minute in years. But chronometers are not made of
material utterly imperishable; which are wholly imper-
vious to the changes of heat and cold. Possibly a chronometer may fail at last, may fail a man in an emergency,
in a case of life and death. But a man's ethical consciousness is liable to fail him at any time; in any case
in which he is interested.

Take the case of St. Peter, when the Saviour took the
disciples and began to tell them the strange shadows
which overhung Him in Jerusalem, to which he was going. What said Peter's ethical consciousness to this?
"Be it far from Thee, Lord; this thing shall not be
done unto Thee." This thing was the event which has
since occupied the thought of the world; the event of
which, as we interpret it, skeptical men say: "It is in-
famous to attribute such a thing, the suffering of the innocent for the guilty, to a just God!" This is the way
Peter felt. Peter loved his Lord, even though his love
was so inconstant and passionate. He thought he was

ready to die for Him. And if death had come from
his first sword-stroke he was ready. And under the im-
pulse of his love, Peter's ethical consciousness led him to
remonstrate against his Master's being subjected to suffering. Peter's ethical consciousness was perverted by
his sensibility. The thing against which he remonstrated,
was the most consummate display of God's love.

The great thinker, Coleridge, has said : "If prudence,
though practically inseparable from morality, is not to be
confounded with moral principle, still less may sensibility ; that is, a constitutional quickness of sympathy with
pain and pleasure, and a keen sense of the qualifications
that accompany social intercourse, mutual endearments,
and reciprocal preferences, be mistaken or deemed a substitute for either. Sensibility is not even a sure pledge
of a good heart, though among the most common mean-
ings of that many-meaning and too-commonly mis-
applied expression. So far from being morality, or one
with the moral principle, it ought not even to be placed
in the same rank with prudence. For prudence, at least,
is an offspring of the understanding ; but sensibility, the
sensibility I mean, here spoken of, is for the greater part
a quality of the nerves, and a result of individual bodily
temperament." John Foster had too much sensibility
to be a safe judge as to the nature and duration of future
punishment.

The Saviour teaches that not even the sparrow falleth
to the ground without our Father. And elsewhere we
read that God's tender mercies are over all his works.
Are we to infer from this that if we break or defy the

laws which He has put into the constitution of things we shall not suffer for it?   Apply your ethical consciousness to the Gay Head disaster, where a steamer loaded with passengers just from their homes and almost in sight of them, runs upon a ledge of rocks, and goes to pieces. What message has such an event as this, to those who believe that they can test the doctrines of the Bible, the principles of God's government, by their ethical consciousness?   Is not the same God who is in providence, also in the Bible, in the kingdom of grace?

III.   Holding fast the form of sound works is the only way to mark and insure progress in the truth.   The form of sound words is the way-mark of thought in the advance toward clearer light.

Every now and then a man or a class of men get the idea that they have made a great discovery; are leading off a grand movement.   Like the commander of the awkward squad at an old-fashioned country muster, they give the word of command "Forward, march!" and expect the whole generation of thinkers are following after them, when. lo! upon looking around they are all alone; they are great leaders in epaulettes and feathers, forsooth; but no man follows them!   The first thing that a man has to do who thinks he has made a discovery worthy of being patented; a discovery which all the world will want, is to pore over the files of the Patent Office, to see if some one has not been there before him.   Now we go to the Apostle's Creed, so-called, and find that, according to this symbol, Christ decended into hell; into hades as at first intended, or as Pearson in his work on the Creed makes claim, into the literal grave. If, therefore, there is any progress in the eschatology of the New Movement, it is progress backward ; backward however, not to the primitive churches, but to the middle ages. For, according to Pearson, the primitive churches thought just as Protestant Christendom has thought.

How do we know there has been any advance in any human science ? It is by comparing what was once believed and taught with what is now believed and taught ; that is, the creed of the past with that of the present. There was a time, antecedent to which medical men did not believe in the circulation of the blood in vertebrated animals. There was a time antecedent to which botanists did not believe in the circulation of sap. But there have been no such discoveries in the science of theology. The progress of thought in theological science, in the science of God, has been rather in the art of better stating what the Bible teaches and the relations of the different parts of the Bible truth. This theory that our ethical conciousness shall determine what is ethical truth fit for God to reveal, is not in the line of theological progress. Theological progress, at least in evangelistic schools of thought, has never assumed to eliminate anything which the Bible teaches, on the score that it ought not to be in the Bible. It has treated Revelation reverently, as all true science treats God's works. It has not undertaken to set up a theological orrery and say thus the great planets revolve ; and if they do not, so much the worse for them. God did not make the system ; or, if He did, He is not a God of skill and power and love.

It is a singular illustration of the unanimity of Christian thought during the Christian era, that there are only three grand symbols of doctrine which have been ever adopted by believers. And they are in substance one. There has been activity, movement; but it has been around the same great centres which draw all things toward themselves. And it is because of the unanimity of Christian experience. The ethical character of the Atonement, forensically conceived and stated, may be as directly and summarily defined from Christian experience as in another way. Here is a sinner; no longer a philosopher, no longer a theologian. How does it affect the heart of this man to be told that the Son of God, who knew no sin, became sin for him? It is Saul of Tarsus; not philosophizing, but repenting, blindly feeling after God, if perhaps he may find him; finding no place for the sole of his feet in that horrible pit and miry clay, till he comes to the thought, which he afterwards expressed for all ages: "God commendeth His love to us, in that while we were yet sinners, Christ died for us." There is a moment when the ethical consciousness of a sinner is prepared to see God in Christ Jesus, reconciling the world unto Himself, and to find beauty in Him, such that He is desirable. And as it is with Paul, so it is with Augustine, so it is with you and me.

No army can move safely without carrying its impedimenta; its things that hinder; its commissariat with it. The impedimenta of the great army of God moving on into the ages is the truth as it is experienced. The form of sound words is dear indeed, because hallowed by sacred memories; because confessed by ancestors, which it has inspired; it is dear, because we have confessed it; but it is especially dear, because it is equally written upon the tablet of our hearts; and we know that God has revealed it to us by His Spirit.   There is no sense in which it is true that God's Spirit is moving upon the hearts of men, to reveal to them new religious truth. God's Spirit is an interpreter.   He shows us, in our hearts, what God means in the Bible.   But our Christian experience is in no proper sense a new revelation.   It is the old revelation, with foot-notes, written by the hand that for our offence was nailed to the Cross.   It is the old revelation, with addenda and appendices, which are personal to us.

The holding fast of the form of sound words, my brethren, is sometimes looked at as a light matter.   Some hold them fast; others let them go, and are glad to get rid of them.   People in these days pay a premium to the man who calls himself liberal.   Liberal of what? Liberal of the truth as God has declared it, and as the saints of all ages have believed it!   What right has any man to give away what does not belong to him; what belongs only to God?   Liberal indeed!   As though it were a matter of indifference, or a matter of taste, or a matter of convenience, or a matter of society.   Liberal of what God teaches us to hold fast!   Why, the more of God's truth a man gives away, the more he gives himself away; the more he destroys himself.   Man lives not by bread alone, but by every word that proceedeth out of the mouth of God.   It is not for us to believe as

little as we can, but as much as we can, of the truth that
God has taught.   This is what makes us children of
God; rooted and grounded in God, and thoroughly
furnished for the work of God !

> Faith of the fathers !   Hold it fast,
>   Though foe on foe assail it ;
> 'Twas wrought 'neath persecution's blast,
>   Shall martyrs' children fail it?
>
> Faith of the fathers!   Be it mine,
>   Against all odds to hold it ;
> Sealed with their blood, as truth divine,
>   And told as they have told it.
>
> Faith of the fathers !   Hand it down
>   To latest generation,
> One God, one Lord, one cross, one crown,
>   One free and full salvation !
>
> Faith of the fathers !   It shall stand
>   At that last day appalling ;
> When at the Judge's great command
>   The worlds, like leaves, are falling.
>
> Faith of the fathers !   On that day
>   One word that Christ has spoken,
> Though heaven and earth shall pass away,
>   One word shall not be broken !

III.

THE RACE SOLVENT.

COLOSSIANS III: II. "Where there is neither Greek nor Jew, circumcision nor uncircumcision, barbarian, Scythian, bond nor free; but Christ is all, and in all."

The old alchemists believed that there was a universal solvent, which would transmute the baser metals into gold; that they could reduce them all down to one base, and that would be gold. It was a visionary dream. It was the delusion of a day. And yet it bore the burden of a great truth; of the greatest truth. Humanity, in its race differences and antagonisms; in its prejudices; in its class-competitions and caste-abominations, is like these baser metals. It needs some universal solvent to bring out its gold. Even its religions have only multiplied and intensified these differences. There is no odium like the odium theologicum. There is no contempt for the publican, ay, for ordinary humanity, like the contempt of the Pharisee; the separated one, ay, the one most separated to God, the Father of us all. In the apostle's day the Jew despised the Greek; the Greek the Jew. The world was full of divisions ethnic, race-divisions, divisions civil, divisions social. Every

thing that keeps men from each other keeps them from
God. The Hebrew mistook and misinterpreted his relation to man because of his relation to God, thinking
that the drawing by which he was drawn to God was
centrifugal toward humanity; drew him out of humanity's circles, not finding out that the nearer a man comes
to God the nearer he is to every creature of God; and
that we cannot love Him, who begat, without loving the
humblest ever begotten of Him, and that the Divine
Fatherhood of God implies as its complement the universal brotherhood of man.

The fathers of this Republic; great men, wise men;
began their immortal work at the throne of God as a
Creator. This was their point of departure : God the
Creator; man the creature. Because man had one Creator, and because with Him was no respect of persons,
they proclaimed all men free and equal and entitled to
certain rights which could not be alienated ; which they
took with them wherever they went. And, yet, from a
certain class, before one hundred years had elapsed, this
great, free people had legislated away every one of these
rights. There were three millions of God's creatures
among them who had been stolen from their native
Africa, and who had been robbed of every right which
had come from God; who had not a right which they
were bound to respect. They were transported across
the great seas like cattle ; they were sold on the auction-
block ; they were stripped of their children, and the earth
was dumb, and the very heavens seemed brass to their

petitions. Then came the thunder-peal of God's judg-
ments; then came the lightning character of His wrath.
We heard, we saw, and we trembled. Then came our
great moral awakening. We listened to the voice of
God. And, upon our knees; the enemy's cannon still
ringing in our ears, and their bayonets still flashing their
fateful light in our eyes; we said to God, we said to the
whole civilized world: "We have been very guilty
concerning our brother; we took off his birth-right coat
and parted it among us; we cast him into that pit;
we sold him to those slave-merchants; we sent him
down to Egypt; we hurt his feet with fetters; we stripped him of every right which God had given him; the
right to self, to wife, to children, to property, to country,
to God." We said, also, to him: "This warfare we
are waging is not for ourselves; it is for humanity; come
into it like a man and a brother and share the results;
take this gun; put on this uniform; stand side by side
with us; go with us down into that valley of death, and
when the conflict is over, share with us equally the right
which God has given you; of which we have so cruelly
dispossessed you." And he who had been praying and
waiting so long, he thought we meant it; he took us at
our word.

But how is it to-day? Citizenship to him means
living under a flag which cannot protect him in
the enjoyment of his civil and political rights; a flag
which sweetly beckoned him to the battle-field, and now
flaps its folds in weakness over him. We say: "You,

who were once entertained at first-class hotels and rode
in first-class cars for your masters' sakes, and society took
no offence; the Government which took you from the
hands of your masters in arms to destroy it, cannot help
you. Go back to the ante-bellum period; your citizenship a mockery and disgrace; not serfs in name, but
pariahs in fact. This is what we now conclude to be
the meaning of our contract with our brother in black.
This is our sober second thought, as we wrap ourselves
in our judicial robes of silk. We, every one of whose
steps to any high position, civil and social, has been a
step which has been born of resistance to oppression,
and has been purchased with blood. We take back the
hand we stretched out to our brother in the day of our
distress, for him to help us, and leave him to struggle
there in the horrible pit and the miry clay into which
slavery dragged him; a citizen of the United States, and
yet not a citizen of the several States thereof. Well,
probably it is best so.

Doubtless, politics is not the universal solvent. Our
fathers tried it, and it failed them. We have tried it
with the same result. It promises more than it ever performs. When France dismantled her churches and
boasted that she had a better gospel than they had given
her; when she abolished the Lord's day and divided the
weeks into tens instead of sevens; when her wild citi-
zens, drunk with the blood of kings and nobles, like so
many demons, sang the Marseillaise in her barricaded
streets, she thought the millennium had dawned. But

the light of that day was the lurid light of the pit. It was all done in the name of liberty and equality. God was gone, religion was gone. All that France needed was citizenship. It was only the oppressed rising up in a paroxysm of power to wreak themselves on their long-time oppressors ; it was only the tyranny of the people versus the tyranny of the kings ; the people crowding into days the vengeance of centuries. It has become very plain in these latter days that a true republic is impossible without a Christian basis. The Deistic basis is not enough ; least of all the Atheistic. There needs to be not only a God and Father, but a God-Man who is God and brother. And the subject which I shall discuss this morning, is

THE CROSS OF CHRIST THE ONLY SOLVENT FOR RACE DIFFERENCES.

"Where there is neither Greek nor Jew, circumcision nor uncircumcision, barbarian, Scythian, bond nor free; but Christ is all, and in all."

1. The Cross of Christ proves man's universal brotherhood. If He is our Brother-man we are His brother-men. Our Revolutionary fathers thought creation proved man's universal brotherhood. This is the gospel of the Declaration. It proves it just as creation proves a God : only to the Christian mind. Every Christian finds the Creator in creation ; every Christian finds his brother-man in the created, just in proportion as he is a Christian. For nearly one hundred years this nation did not find a brother-man in a creature of God. It found

only a human chattel, to be bought and sold. Not until Christ has anointed his blind eyes with eye-salve, does man in the pride of race, of birth, of culture, in his carnal aristocracy; which is just as carnal as any other carnal thing, though he is often very proud of it; actually assent to the truth that the most degraded of human beings has a right to call him brother-man ; has a right to his sympathy and help as a brother-man; to give him signals of distress, as though he belonged to the same guild. He admits the fact, but he does not enact it.

Terence, who had been a slave, could put it into his drama, " Nothing which concerns man is foreign to me." It is a negative statement, like all pagan sentiments of humanity; like Confucius' negative of the golden rule. It remained for a nobler Roman than he, who did not write dramas, to be cheered by the Roman populace, but who, in the great world-drama, higher than that of which Shakespeare writes in the prologue to Henry V. :

> " A kingdom for a stage, princes to act,
> And monarchs to behold the swelling scene ;"

it remained for a nobler Roman, in the great world-drama, of which the author of the Epistle to the Hebrews speaks, when he reminds us that we are compassed about by a cloud of witnesses unseen ; a nobler Roman than he, to put it, pulsating with his own life-blood, interpreted beyond the possibility of mistake, into human history, into the history of the kingdom of God. "Who is weak, and I am not weak ? Who is offended, and I burn not ?" Brand another man and you brand me.

Where did he learn this? At the feet of Gamaliel? At the feet of Gamaliel he learned quite another gospel. He learned to glory not in infirmities but in advantages. He learned to glory in that high plane of privilege, on which he walked as a Jew; in the adoption, in the giving of the law, in the promises; just as many of us have gloried in the battles of freedom, civil and religious, in the old world and the new; in the prowess of the Anglo-Saxon name, and in the red-hot currents which flow in the Anglo-Saxon blood, rather than in our infirmities for the Indian, the African, the Asiatic. For here was a man who could ride down his feeble and innocent fellow-creatures on horseback, like a true knight of ku-klux-ism. And precisely such a man, Jesus of Nazareth found him, on the way to Damascus. Where did he learn this: "Who is weak and I am not weak? Who is offended, and I burn not?" He learned it where only it is to be learned. Not in French politics! No! Not in American politics; but at the feet of Him who for our offences was nailed to the Cross of Calvary. Those feet were maimed with nails by this principle. It was not in Gamaliel; it was not in his own Judaism, or Pharisaism; it was not in pagan civilization; it was only in Him, who can be touched with the feeling of our infirmities; in Him, who, when He thought it not robbery to be equal with God, took the form of a servant and sanctified it forevermore; and being found in fashion as a man, humbled himself and became obedient unto death, even the death of the cross.

When we take this bread and drink this wine what do we do? We symbolize Christ's human brotherhood. This he did for humanity's sake. What taint of Judaism had He? What recognition did He ever make that He belonged to any single nationality? to any single tribe? to any single class? Is he Brother-man to the Jew only, because he was born of a Jewish mother? Is he any less Brother-man to the Gentile? to the Greek? to the Roman? to the barbarian? to the Scythian? to the bond? to the free? When we eat this bread we eat that which sets forth, what? God manifest in the flesh; God manifest in the flesh of humanity. Not because we are Anglo-Saxon, and have the Anglo-Saxon Bible, the Anglo-Saxon literature, the Anglo-Saxon civilization, the Anglo-Saxon freedom and manhood, of which we are so proud, have you and I a claim to this Brother-Man. It is because we are on the same human level with the other races, from which we so much differ, and above which God has given us such an exaltation. For such were we. It is because we are brother-men to Frederick Douglass, and Sitting Bull, and the lost Chinaman, who has been smuggled from the Celestial Kingdom because this continent is too narrow for him and us. It is because we are so low, and not because we are so high, that we have a right to sit here, to eat this bread, and to drink this cup. This broken bread is the emblem, not of Anglo-Saxon humanity, but of lost, degraded, fallen humanity.

II. The Cross of Christ interprets man's universal

brotherhood. It needs to be interpreted. It is the last thing that man learns here; that in Christ Jesus the humblest man is his equal.

Ask almost any man if he wants the elevation of his brother-man; if he wants his brother-man in India, in China, in Japan, in the South, on the Pacific coast, made his equal; ay, given a chance to outstrip him in the struggle for betterment; and he will usually answer, "Why, yes, of course. Do I not pray for it and contribute for it?" But will you sacrifice your prejudices for his sake? He needs different religious influences; different educational influences; different social influences; he needs to feel that he is no longer ostracised, and that he may aspire for himself and his children, just as you may. Will you adopt him into your religious, educational, social circles? But you reply: "That is a society question." It is a society question, and you belong to the kingdom of God; to the unseen society, which, by the power of His Cross, this God-Man, who took the form of a servant, is gathering out of the nations. You have fellowship with Him in His humiliation for humanity's sake. And yet you propose to decide this question according to the laws and usages of a society to which you do not belong, out of which God has called you, and against whose inhumanity to man, against whose worldly pride the Cross is a standard lifted up by God Himself. You are under the most sacred of bonds to record your testimony as belonging to quite other society. In what sense, after all, are we brothers?

Can society answer this question? . Can anything but
the Cross of Christ? The Saviour gives us a picture of
what it is to be a true neighbor, in the parable of the
Good Samaritan. "Who, asks He, was neighbor to him
that fell among thieves?" He that thought it was a society question, a question of caste? He who came and
looked on him and passed by on the other side? He that
put money into the contribution-box for him, or sent
some one else to help him to the hospital? No, only the
man that set him upon his own beast, carried him to an
inn, and took care of him. By the same law human
brotherhood, as the Cross interprets it, means more than
good wishes; means more than "Be ye warmed and
filled." It means, in our place and according to our
measure, taking upon ourselves the burdens and dis-
abilities under which our brother-man, of whatever
station, of whatever nationality, is seen to labor, and
trying, personally, to relieve him. If he is ignorant
of books we want to teach him books; if he is ignorant
of God we want to give him a knowledge of God. If
he is stripped of his rights and immunities we want to
stand for him and to lift up our testimony against the out-
rage. A man cannot live a neighbor to man, if he is
not living a neighbor to God, as He is in Christ Jesus.

Before the war there was organized a benevolent society, whose anniversary occurs the present week; a society to preach the Gospel among the heathen.* Its foun-
ders said: "We cannot take money that has been coined

*American Missionary Association.

from slave labor. It is the price of innocent blood. It cries up to God for vengeance. It is the price of violating the tenderest of human ties ; the most sacred ; of trafficking in the bodies and souls of men. We cannot touch it. We dare not bring it to God's altar as an offering. We dare not go with it in our hands to labor in other lands. The very heathen would spit upon it ; would spurn us." It seemed to a great many that they were straining a point; that they were visionary people. Ah! they saw Him, who is invisible ; Him who will say : "Inasmuch as ye did it unto one of the least." They were only remembering those in bonds as bound with them ; as branded with them. They were only illustrating their sense of the brotherhood of man as taught at the Cross. What is the history of that society? Why, the smoke of our civil contest had hardly cleared away before it began to build up the waste places of the South ; heaping coals of fire upon the people there. Under their auspices, the choicest daughters of New England, as though they had been angels of God, went down there with the spelling-book and the Bible ; took their share of the ostracism meted out to the recent bondsmen for Jesus' sake. Many of them laid down their lives there. There has scarcely been a foreign missionary field in the world which has had more perils, which has demanded greater sacrifices, which has developed spirits more heroic, more Christlike. The same spirit which led our brave boys to die, to make men free, led their sisters to die, to make them holy.

And what do you see to-day? This society has done
more to stay the tide of illiteracy, to lay the foundations
of permanent civil and religious prosperity than all the
other agencies put together. God's secret is with them
that fear Him. The men who for Christ's sake said: "We
cannot set apart to God that which has come from un-
paid human labor; we cannot thus have fellowship with
the works of darkness;" these men God has put into
the forefront of the great battle with ignorance and degradation; the great battle in which the South begins to
ask the nation, which cannot protect the black man, to
come to her help. They got their baptism at the foot
of the Cross. Look at the queenly institutions which
they have planted; look at the thousands of the sons
and daughters of Ethiopia, whom they have developed
in the mental, moral and spiritual stature of true manhood; whom they have polished after the similitude of
a palace; fitted for professions, for business, for home-
life. Look at the churches they have planted. This is
their conception of the brotherhood of man as they have
been taught it at the Cross; as the Cross has interpreted
it to them.

Why is it that you and I have such different standards
for what is heroic in ourselves, and what is heroic in our
foreign missionaries? The foreign missionaries do the
very things at which we are most reluctant. They live
with the heathen: they go down upon their hands and
knees and crawl into their huts. Tenderly brought up
at home, having received the best of modern culture,

fitted to shine in the most refined. circles, they ostracise
themselves; they confront the caste-spirit of heathendom;
nay, of lost humanity; and, perhaps, lay down their lives
there ; and their dust moulders back to dust in those lands
of midnight. Why does the Christian Church at home
calendar. their name as saintly, as Christlike? That man,
David Livingstone, who buried himself in the heart of
Africa, as men let themselves down into the mouth of a
pit where there is fire-damp and death, to save the lost
there, while the civilized world paused in suspense to
know whether he was dead or alive ; whose companions
and protectors were for months and years only wild
Africans; jogging along with his ox-cart, the ark of
Ethiopian civilization ; or borne in his feebleness, on the
shoulders of the men whom his likeness to Christ had
touched to tender issues ; and dying on his knees an object-
lesson to teach men how they should pray for the heathen;
that man David Livingstone, whose dust the doors of
Westminster Abbey swing back, almost of their own
accord, to receive, and the whole civilized world stand
with heads uncovered as it is let down to lie beside the
dust of the kings and counsellors of the earth; what was
there in him that we so much honor ? It was his baptism
into the spirit of his Master, as to lost humanity ; as to the
black continent of Africa. It was his stretching himself upon the form of that dead continent, as the prophet
stretched himself upon the form of the dead child of the
widow of Sarepta, until life came down from God to
reanimate it. And yet, you and I do not know whether

it is quite the thing to teach in a negro Sunday-school; whether we may not stain our immaculate Christianity by sitting in the same pew with an African in God's house; whether our children may not catch the contagion of heathenism by being taught in the same day schools! And this is in Christian America!

III. The Cross of Christ inspires man to acts of universal brotherhood.

Poets sing about it; politicians and statesmen prognostigate it; but nothing else inspires it but the Cross of Christ. And modern civilization, tested by this test, shows what it owes to Jesus Christ, and Him crucified. Modern civilization is a movement toward the prevalence, all over the earth, of the sentiment of human brotherhood. Just think how near we are together; how we can almost whisper into each other's ears. Shall we, in spiritual things, be behind the movement of modern material communication? behind steam, the telegraph, the telephone? Already men talk seriously of reaching the Old World; great, sluggish Asia herself; across the American Continent and Behring's Strait. "And there shall be no more sea." And yet races are divided as if by impassable seas.

I do not find fault with the letter of the decision of the Supreme Court.* I am disappointed; I am grieved to see law interpeted as against freedom. I presume, however, the court has only intended to affirm the facts as they exist. Doubtless, the tendency of American

*Civil Rights Decision.

progress is to try to cure everything by legislation. We are in too much haste to stop for education; we say, "Give us a law!" But law is always weak through the flesh. It is never strong, except as the spirit is with us. And to-day, as we stand under the shadow of the Cross, I appeal to a higher court; I remind myself, I remind you, that from the Cross itself; from our Elder Brother hanging there for humanity's sake; and not from the Declaration of Independence; and not from constitutional amendments; not from French republicanism, and not from American republicanism, I derive the law of universal brotherhood. I see it in the print of the nails and the spear. I see it in the crown of thorns. It is a law as wide as the earth's surface. It is on the land; it is on the deep. It reaches to heaven itself. It reaches to that world where men walk in the light of God; where all earthly differences and distinctions will vanish with the earthly surroundings from which we are liberated; with the robe of flesh which we put off. Think you there is a whiter soul gone up from the communion of this church than that of John H. Cook? Earthly prejudice was silent in his presence. He had more white clients than colored. And when it was announced to the judge of the court, where he practiced, that he was incurably sick, for a moment the course of justice was arrested in its progress, and while he was still living the judge pronounced his eulogy.

In the work that is before us as a Christian people, we shall need the inspiration of this law of human brotherhood. Let us look at it. It is a work that must be done under the force of this law. It is too great for any other motive. In discussing the lessons of the last census, at the recent Inter-State Convention at Louisville, Dr. Waite, of the Census Bureau, stated that the illiteracy of the South had increased in the ten years from 1870-1880, one-half million. That is, that there are one-half million more illiterates than in 1870. Dr. Curry, of Richmond, the superintendent of the Peabody fund, said at the same convention, that to-day 30 per cent. of the white and 70 per cent. of the negro population of the South are illiterate, and that the only solution of the race problem in this country is the school and the church. And he makes a strong appeal, like the long roll-call of an army, to the national government to rise up, and by giving national aid to, the cause of education, save the Republic. Dr. Haygood, another Southern gentleman, says: "The colored man never will have his best chance there till the reign of the Gospel and common sense." This is what I am pleading for. These people; who multiply themselves by ten every one hundred years; Dr. Haygood says they have done that in the last century; if we can find no place for them in the school-houses and the churches; in the inns, the cars, and the steamboats; are bound to have the largest share in the population of the South. Yes, and in its illiteracy, too. They rise up like a great black cloud in the horizon, and if Howard University, and Fiske University, and Hampton Institute; if the

Christian schools and churches of the South; if the churches and other benevolent agencies of the North, with their millions a year, for the last twenty years, have thus far been fighting a losing battle with illiteracy there, the nation may find that though she is so little a nation that she has no power to protect her colored citizen in his political and civil rights, she will require to assume some of the prerogatives of a nation in order to protect herself against his illiteracy!

One fearful element in the problem before us is the fact that the illiterate persons of the South are largely colored women. The mothers of the children, the home-educators, they who give direction to the school or from the school; to the church or from it; these are the majority of illiterate ones! If there is any department of work for the colored people, which deserves emphasis, it is this. " What is wanting," said Napoleon, one day to Madame Campan, " in order that the youth of France be well educated?" " Good mothers!" was the reply. " An ounce of mother," said another, " is worth a pound of clergy." And another still, " The mother's heart is the child's school-room."

But love of country is not an undying love. If there be patriotism, it shall fail. Appalled by the desolations, wearied with the weaknesses, impatient with the inconsistencies and unreasonablenesses of this race when the war ended, but little above heathenism, the patriot makes a law, gives his mite through the Freedman's Bureau and

turns away.   But not so the Christian.   If there be love
of country and country's ideals, it shall fail.   The time
comes when the Declaration of Independence con-
tains glittering generalities.   If there be love of humanity, it shall fail.   The time comes, when for humanity's
sake, man thinks he has done enough.   But love for
Christ never faileth.   The more a man does for Christ's
sake, the more he can do; the more he gives, the more
he can give; the more he bears, the more he can bear.
This world is to be redeemed, by introducing the life of
its redeemed ones into its life; as Christ's life has been
introduced into them.   It is to be made one in Christ
Jesus, by the solvent of the Cross.   Just as the life of the
spirit does not belong to space or time; has no period,
no nationality, no clime; so the love of the spirit.   It si
for the spirit, and not for its investiture.   It is for the
image of God in man; it is for the citizen of the Republic of God, which is coming down from Him to meet
us.

My brethren in the Lord, when we seat ourselves
around the Master's table this morning let us come not
as Greek and Jew, circumcised and uncircumcised, barbarian, Scythian, bond and free; but as those to whom
Christ is all, and in all; as those who bear each other's
burdens; who burn at each other's wrongs; who sympa-
thize with each other's sorrows; whose faith and hope,
whose joys and sorrows, are one and make them one in
the Lord Jesus.

I know no differences of race,
   Of African and Saxon;
Of tawny skin, of rose-checked face,
   Of hair or crisp or flaxen.
The soul within, that is the man,
   There is God's image hidden!
And there He looks, each guest to scan,
   The bidden and unbidden.

In Jesus Christ are all men one,
   And He their Elder Brother;
The races, various, 'neath the sun,
   Why should they vex each other?
Or Jew, or Greek, the blood the same
   Within their veins that's flowing;
Or bond or free, to all He came,
   His dying love bestowing.

The same, the bread, His flesh we break.
   The wine, His blood, we're pouring;
We lose ourselves here for His sake,
   Repenting and adoring.
There are no differences of grace,
   God's love to all descending;
The humblest is His dwelling place,
   His wing the least defending.

What though my brother-man has worn
   The bondman's yoke and fetter,
The scoff and jeer of pride has borne;
   I am the more his debtor!
What man is weak and I'm not weak?
   Offended, I'm not burning?
Is dumb and I refuse to speak?
   Is spurned, take not the spurning?

One God in love, broods over all!
　One prayer to Him is taught us;
One name for mercy when we call,　.
　One ransom Christ has brought us.
One heart of meekness, lowly mind,
　Life's counter currents breasting;
One Father's house we hope to find,
　Within God's bosom resting.

IV

LIFE ETERNAL.

JOHN XVII, 3 : " And this is life eternal, that they might know Thee, the only true God, and Jesus Christ whom Thou hast sent."

This is a definition of eternal life from the lips of the Lord Jesus Christ, and addressed to His Father and to our Father. Never were words spoken in circumstances more solemn, more tender. Before His awe-struck disciples He stands there, negotiating with the unseen Partner of the mysterious transaction, which is about to be consummated. The hour is come. For this cause came He into the world, that He might impart life eternal to as many as would receive Him. But what is life eternal? He answers this for the sake of His disciples, for our sakes, upon whom these ends of the world have come. " And this is life eternal, that they might know Thee, the only true God, and Jesus Christ, whom Thou hast sent.'

This is something different from immortality. The doctrine of immortality is that the soul will never cease to exist, that death does not end it, that death is only an invisible bridge over which it passes to a state beyond. This is a doctrine of natural religion. The Bible does not so much reveal it as take it for granted. The existence of God is a doctrine of natural religion. That there is a hereafter, and that every living being will have part in it; that there is a God and that every creature of His shall give account to Him ; of these things, we have witness within ourselves. We have an instinct which leads us to believe them. "We are better believers in immortality," says Emerson, " than we can give grounds for;" and, says James Martineau, "we do not believe immortality, because we have proved it, but we forever try to prove it because we believe it." But what is called life eternal is a different thing from immortality. Life eternal is something which is revealed as possible to those who are immortal. If the doctrine of immortality is assumed as the very basis of a revelation, is taken for granted by God in communicating to man His will, the laws that should guide him, and the motives that should move him, the doctrine of life eternal is a doctrine of revealed religion. "Who abolished death and brought life and immortality to light in the Gospel?" In other words, let light in upon life and immortality.

LIFE ETERNAL :

Let this be the subject of the morning's discourse.

I. If there is such a thing as life eternal, it must be derived directly from God. God is the only being who has eternal life, either for Himself or any of His creatures. Temporal life we derive from temporal parentage. Eternal life we must derive from parentage eternal. " That which is born of the flesh is flesh, and that which is born

of the Spirit is spirit." There was a time when it was
proclaimed by modern science that dead matter has the
power to beget living things; in other words, that life
is spontaneously generated by death. But this is no
longer proclaimed. The present doctrine of science is:
"Life only from life." There is an impassable gulf between the not-living and the living; a gulf which can
be bridged only by creative power, that is, God.

"Marvel not that I said unto ye, ye must be born
again." The birth spoken of here by the Saviour is
into life eternal. We have had earthly parents. They
have given us this pleasing, anxious being; and they have
passed away. We who have derived this being from them
shall likewise pass away. The Saviour teaches us that
our earthly entrance into life bears the burden of another
entrance; that as we are born of man so we need be born
of God! Temporal parentage gives us temporal life;
eternal parentage, life eternal. This doctrine is one of
the hard doctrines of the Bible; one of the distasteful
ones. The children of Adam do not like to be told of
a new stock better than theirs. The Bible teaches that
until born again we are dead to God; alienated from
Him; dead to the spiritual world; alienated from it.
The men who wish to get the supernatural out of religion
have been bent upon doing what modern science has
tried, and tried in vain. They have been trying to get
life out of not-life; life out of death; regeneration out
of culture.

Recall some of the futile efforts of modern science to

evolve life out of dead matter. Dr. Bastian, for example, after repeated experiments, announced that he had succeeded. But Professor Tyndall, more carefully repeating similar experiments, found that Dr. Bastian had left germs of living things in the air within the flasks with which he experimented. And Mr. Dallinger proved that the lower forms of life are capable of surviving higher temperatures than Dr. Bastian had applied for their annihilation, so that both Professors Huxley and Tyndall fully admit that thus far there is "no experimental testimony to prove that life ever appears independent of antecedent life." This is the very law of Revelation respecting spiritual things. Christ appears here among men, a new type of man, coming to do the Father's will in His life and death; withstanding the evil that is in the world. And when Nicodemus approaches Him by night, and proposes to adopt Him as a teacher come from God, proposes to submit himself as a pupil to His teachings, to make culture a substitute for regeneration, the Saviour thrusts into his face the doctrine that new life is what he wants. "Rabbi, we know Thou art a teacher come from God." This Nicodemus. Jesus answered and said unto Him: "Except a man be born of water and of the Spirit, he cannot enter the Kingdom of God." Not that Jesus implied that he was not a teacher come from God, but that man wants something antecedent to teaching before he can be a fit pupil for such a teacher. His type of men cannot be repeated here without the new birth.

There is a way of receiving God through the senses; through sights and sounds; as we see and hear manifestations of His power and Godhead. You begin with your little child, and tell her that the thunder is the voice of God; that He kindles the stars in the night; that He touches the trees and they bud; the grass and it blooms. There is a way of receiving God through the reason; by thinking of Him, and inferring His existence, as a matter of philosophy, in order better to explain our theory of the universe. Unrenewed man is competent to either of these two processes. They do not involve allegiance to God! This is not the knowledge of God, which is the condition of life eternal. "That they might know Thee, the only true God, and Jesus Christ, whom Thou hast sent."

The knowledge of God in Jesus Christ, who came here to reveal Him, awakens man to a new life; gives him new thoughts, new emotions, new motives, new aims. We talk about the dead languages; meaning the languages of dead nations; languages unspoken by living men and women. But there are scholars to whom no language is dead; every language embalms the soul of those who once spoke it. How many words have come into the English through Greek or Latin embalmment! But, languages are dead, also, because they no longer speak to the living. And here it is the living men who are dead, and not the languages. The Greek of Demosthenes, was this ever dead to Rufus Choate? It is not the words of God that are dead; it is the men to whom they are addressed. It is not the motives of the Bible that are dead; it is the men to whom they are addressed. It is not the influences of the Spirit which are dead, but the men to whom they are addressed. I read to you in the Greek the passage: "Behold, I stand at the door, and knock!" but your ear is dead to it. The words are just as full of the life of God, and the yearning of God's love as though I read the English. The language of the Spirit is Greek to men unrenewed. The difference between people is, that some of them want to know God in creation; and some in philosophy; while the only true knowledge of Him is in Christ Jesus, who has come as a mediator between God and man; as a propitiation for the sins of the whole world. And this knowledge is life eternal.

There are men and women here this morning who have tried again and again to awaken in themselves this life eternal; to get life out of death. They have yearned for God as a comforter in their troubles; for a helper in their weaknesses; for a counsellor in their ignorance. And they have tried to break through their materialism; the wall of sense by which they are surrounded, by which they seemed walled in, and get at spiritual things, so that they may be real to them; so that they may never return to their previous life. But, having no hold upon God by faith; feeling none of the pulsations of a new life beating within their souls, they have soon become impatient at their failures and weaknesses and gone back to the old life of sense. The Saviour does not say,

"'Except a man be born of water and of the Spirit,''
because there is anything arbitrary or artificial here.
It is because "'Life can come only from life !'" He
does not say it, because He wants to hinder men from
coming into God's kingdom ; but to show them how to
get in. Teaching alone will not do it. It is helpful.
But life is absolutely necessary.

II. If there is such a thing as life eternal it must have a
suitable environment : that is, a suitable setting ; air to
breathe ; circumstances where it can feed itself and protect itself, and prolong itself, or be fed ; protected and
prolonged by its author.

"'The new creature,'" spoken of in the Bible as the
result of regeneration, is like all other creatures of God
in this : that in order to live, it must have adapted to it
conditions appropriate to its life ; must have its habitat.
In its birth, we have its nature ; in its environment, its
circumstances, we have all the rest we need in order to
determine what will come of it. If it have life, and
an eternal environment suited to this life, it will live
forever. The influence of climate upon animal and
vegetable life, is one of the most interesting depart-
ments of natural science. In his great work, the Kos-
mos, Humboldt has classified the animal and vegetable
life, so that we see how the law of unity runs through
the whole system of creation. In the same latitudes ;
in different latitudes, with the same temperature, we
have the same or similar plants and trees; the same, or
similar animals. This, notwithstanding the provision

that God has made for the transportation of plant and
tree germs on the wings of the wind ; notwithstanding the
force of locomotion in animals. Only those organic
structures, whether vegetable or animal, which get life
and a start in a new habitat, only those to which the
habitat is adapted, which are adapted to it, can long survive.

This new life of the soul, which is called in the Saviour's terminology, in the terminology of the Bible, life
eternal must have its habitat, or it will not survive. It
comes only from God; it lives only in God, and in
those who are surrounded by God as a renewing Spirit.
It is a brave plant, the edelweiss, that blooms among
the eternal snows of the Alps, that looks out in its
fragile feebleness and beauty upon those unbroken solitudes of God, and is at home there. But it is just so
with the edelweiss of the soul, the white flower of faith.
It gets its nourishment out of God's highest fastnesses.
It is a brave tree, the fir-tree, that goes climbing up the
mountain peaks, like a scaling party up the ramparts,
which are crowned with eternal silence and death. But
that is its habitat. There it lifts up its Gothic spire, as
though to remind us that the earth itself is God's cathe-
dral ; there it murmurs with the same deep voice that
the ocean has ; breathing into God's ear its hymnal of
praise.

When we read, " Whom God loveth He chasteneth,
and scourgeth every son He receiveth ;" and again, "If ye
endure chastening, God dealeth with you as sons;" we get

some suggestions as to the habitat of the soul in which this eternal life has been awakened. It is like the habitat of the edelweiss and the fir, in high up solitudes of faith. This sonship spoken of here is the sonship of God; describes the new life of the soul in the likeness of God. The Being, bearing human form, who once walked among men, illustrating this life eternal, what was His habitat, His environment? He was a man of sorrows, and acquainted with grief. But, only this, because it was the Father's will! The Father's will was His habitat, His environment. Walking among us He breathed the air of eternity. He climbed the mountains, He penetrated solitudes, to get away from things of time and sense, and be with God. On the mount of trans figuration, the three favored disciples saw what com panionship He had; what air He breathed; how time and eternity met in Him, and in what He was doing.

The Saviour says, "If a man abide not in Me, he is cast forth as a branch, and is withered." "Without Me, out of connection with Me, ye can do nothing." The soul has its habitat, its environment, the soil in which it is rooted and grounded, in God; in God manifest in the flesh! If it have such a habitat, what can happen to it, that will be for its injury? "Who shall separate us from the love of Christ? Shall tribulation, or distress, or persecution, or famine, or nakedness, or peril, or sword? Nay, in all these things we are more than conquerors through Him that loved us. For I am persuaded that "neither death nor life, nor angels, nor principalities, nor powers, nor things present, nor things to come, nor height nor depth, nor any other creature, shall be able to separate us from the love of God, which is in Jesus Christ, our Lord.'' The fish has its habitat, the water, where it glides gracefully and lives joyously; where its proper food swims or floats around it. The bird has its habitat, the air, where it wings its pathway at will; where it mounts, where it descends, where it sails. The animal, man, has his habitat, the earth; creation's vast storehouse; where he is at liberty to eat what grows spontaneously, or what he can make grow; to fabricate what he chooses to live in, and to wear. The water and the air are not his habitat; but the solid earth.

But, earth and earthly things are just as little the habitat of the soul of man of this life eternal, as the air and the water, of his body. His soul lives here, because of its relation to his body; looks out as from the gratings of a prison-house. Three-score years and ten are allotted to him, for the life of his body; and then the connection between them is broken; and he, who had heaven begun within him, mounts up to heaven, and to God. It is a fight with the surrounding conditions to make trees live in some of our territories. The Agricultural Department is querying whether trees, such as grow in some of the drier and colder regions of Russia, will not thrive in Dakota. It is a fight to maintain the life of God in the soul of man; to keep its environment what God would have it. But, if this is done, eternal life is just as sure as the present life; be-cause this life having once begun in God, it can never end so long as the soul abides in God.

The question with the man, who has never come into relations with things not seen, in such a sense, that there is a part of his nature, which just as really regards them its habitat, as the other part regards the earth as belonging to it; the question with this man is this: "'Can my inner nature form such correspondences with what is unchangeable and eternal, that when what is changeable and temporal shall have passed away, those correspondences will continue?'' This is the very doctrine of the test. "And this is life eternal, that they might know Thee, the only true God, and Jesus Christ, whom Thou hast sent.'' Modern science has given us this definition of a possible life eternal. It is in the words of Herbert Spencer: "Perfect correspondence would be perfect life. Were there no changes in the environment, but such as the organism had adapted changes to meet; and were it never to fail in the efficiency with which it met them, there would be an eternal existence and eternal knowledge.'' If our souls have perfect correspondence with that which is in its very nature eternal, unchangeable, they must have perfect life in that environment. That this environment can never fail in the efficiency with which it surrounds us, and meets our wants, is as sure as that God is God, and He has revealed Himself in Jesus Christ, His Son.

There is no doubt that there are particulars in which

the soul changes its environment at death. It leaves the·
body. It leaves all the surroundings, the scaffolding of·
circumstances, material, intellectual, spiritual, social, on
which the great Master-Builder has been standing, as the
structure of character has here gone up. The scaffold--
ing of · time and sense, of earthly parenthood, and
human kin is all removed, and what has been
erected remains alone to be inspected by the eye of Him.
who accepts or rejects what has been done here in the
body. Is there an environment which, during the period
of this life, we have made ready, in which to go forth as
we go hence to be here no more? Are there things that
we love, that we feed upon with delight, that inspire us
as thoughts and aspirations, things that relate to God
and the Kingdom of God among men; things that are
more endearing than the earth we tread, and all things
upon it; than the heavens which are arched above us,
with their stars, that seem so imperishable, but which
are to fall like the untimely leaves of the fig tree? Are
there things, such as character, and society, and taste,
and purpose, which, when this earthly environment is
broken up, will fit into, will fit us into that other environment which is the Kingdom of God? These are
questions which do not relate to your religion or my
religion; which is the best? But to the something
deeper, whether we have any religion at all; religion
which will endure when we have no more of its earthly·
forms and props and helps.

III. If there is such a thing as life eternal it cannot be·

maintained without availing itself of the helps of its
suitable environment. There are some men who seem
to think that they can moil here all their lives in the
dirt, and then, at death, fly away a winged soul into all
the delights of paradise! The environment of the grub
is the earth. It is on the earth and of it. And the
grub, which becomes the butterfly, is no more unlike
itself in its grubship when it comes forth from the tomb,
where it has swung insensate, than the new man in Christ
Jesus is like the old man in the image of Adam.

The great function of environment is not to give life;
that only can come from Him who has it to give; nor to
modify life, though incidentally it does this; but to sus-
tain it. The text teaches us that eternal life is to know
God and Jesus Christ, whom He has sent. This defines
it, but it also conditions it. It cannot be maintained
without the fulfilment of this condition. There is no
continued life without environment fitted to the maintenance of this life. Take the sea-gull, that brave pirate
of the wing, that glories in the tempest, and pounces
upon its prey in the water with a sound like th.. .. ;
take the sea-gull and confine him where he can .. ..
only grain diet, and how soon will he pine away and die.
The life of the new-born soul is like God's life, eternal.
But life is only a part of being, when you come to the
question of its continuance. Even life eternal is condi-
tioned on environment, on the soul having its habitat in
God. "Abide in me and I in you!"

The tree, the insect, the bird, the animal finds what

it needs, and thus lives. It is because it does not de-
pend upon its life but uses this life to maintain life.
One of the pitiful stories which come to us from the
Indian country is, that having legislated and betrayed
the wild man out of the lands of his fathers, having
taken him from his native environment, we, who do not
know what to do with our income, let him die of starvation. Once the waters teemed with fish for him, the
woods with venison, the air with fowls. That is the
way the God of nature provided for him. But now our
national Congress votes him his blanket and his rations,
and while he is waiting for it to dispose of more important matters and get to him he dies of starvation.
One great abuse of the doctrine of election is right here :
Men say they have this eternal life and then are careless
about their environment, out of which its maintenance
must spring. Read some of the Psalms. For example,
such passages as these : " He that dwelleth in the secret
place of the Most High shall abide under the shadow
of the Almighty;" " Thou art my hiding place;" " Keep
me as the apple of thine eye, hide me under the shadow
of thy wing ;" " He shall cover thee with His feathers,
and under His wing shall thou trust ; " " Because thou
hast made the Lord, even the Most High, thy habitation.
there shall no evil befall thee, neither shall any plague
come nigh thy dwelling;" "Thou shalt be in league with
the stones of the field, and the beasts of the field shall
be at peace with thee."

Just what the habitat of the creatures of God are to

them; their birth-place, their dwelling-place, their hiding-place; the place that gives them food and drink; just that God is to the life of the believer. The Creator makes no mistake with regard to the habitat of His creatures, the lower animals. When the land-bird wanders off to sea, and with tired and drooping wing strikes at last against the ship's mast, and falls dead to the deck, that is no mistake of the Creator. The dove which the patriarch took back into the window of the ark. sought for her habitat in vain. The waters had not receded from it. But, when a few days later, she came not back again, she had sought and found her habitat. The Creator has made no mistakes with regard to this eternal life. There is only one way of maintaining it. It is by abiding in God and having God's words abide in us.

The text speaks of knowing God as eternal life. In another passage we are exhorted to acquaint ourselves with God and be at peace. This knowledge of God, this acquaintance with Him, is one of the technical things of the Bible. It is not ordinary knowledge; it is experimental. It is not a speaking acquaintance; it is an intimate, familiar, endearing one! Just as the little child knows its tender and patient mother through her ministrations in the nursery and the home; just as the grateful pupil knows the teacher through his wise instructions and counsels; just as the friend knows the friend through his fidelity in the days that try men's souls; so the soul needs to be acquainted with God. Not by the hearing of the ear merely; not through the written word and the church ordinance merely; for these do not bring life eternal! But, when no other eye pities; when no other ear hears; then to go alone to God, as our unfailing friend, to cast ourselves in our helplessness and loneliness upon His care, and feel that He bears us up in His hands; that He regards us in eternal league and covenant with Him; that He puts beneath us the everlasting arms; and that no man is able to pluck us out of His hands; that there is no force in the universe, no foe in the universe to which He has not said: "Touch not mine anointed; those that have made a covenant with Me by sacrifice;" this is life eternal; a life that is imbedded in the very being and attributes of God! Is He omniscient? It is for our sakes. Is He omnipresent? It is to uphold and protect us. Is He omnipotent? We need that omnipotence. With all God's infinite yearnings of love going out after us; with all His attributes engaged for us, we go off into the dread unknown, and to us it is no longer unknown. Knowing God, we are at home in God. No change of being can float us away from Him; can separate us from His life; that life which is hid with Christ in Him. Because He lives, we live also; our life fed from the eternal fountains of His life; forever and forever.

What hast thou done, my soul, to meet
  The destiny impending,
When death's dark vale before thy feet,
  Thou art to it descending?

What hast thou done for that dread hour,
   When heart and flesh shall fail thee?
When burdened with life's deathless dower,
   Those untried scenes assail thee?

Where wilt thou wing thy troubled flight,
   For some safe refuge yearning?
Some shelter from the storm and night,
   To which thou canst be turning?

Where wilt thou go? Where wilt thou dwell?
   Beneath whose shadow hiding?
My soul, in time look to it well,
   Thyself to Christ confiding.

No change of worlds can change His love,
   Nor from that love can sever;
In heights, in depths, beneath, above,
   Thou livest in Him forever!

V.

THE SENSE OF PROPERTY IN SIN.

JOB XIII, 26. "For thou writest bitter things against me, and makest me to possess the iniquities of my youth."

Nothing is more likely to obliterate the sense of sin than the passage of time and the change of standards. It is a very difficult thing for us to realize that our moral lives have an identity like that of our natural ones. The body keeps the scars which were made upon it by the indiscretions of childhood and youth. You look at that right hand of yours. There is where that jackknife slipped as you were shaping a wooden sword, or a wooden spear, or carving out a mimic ship to sail in your mother's wash-tub. You will wear that scar to your grave. It is one of the strange things about this constant flux of the particles of matter in our physical structure, which is just as ceaseless as are the tides of the ocean, that it never disturbs the handwriting of our earlier days; it never disturbs the marks of accident to our various members. The law of identity is a law that, through all this flux of matter, aye, by all this flux of matter, our bodies shall be the same, when we pillow our heads in earth, that they were when first pillowed on a mother's bosom.

It is so of our moral nature. There are multitudes of things which you and I have done, or just escaped doing in our youth, sometimes had it in our hearts to do, which our maturer life severely condemns. We are ashamed of them; they do not seem like us. We look back to such a period where two paths diverged, one leading to wretchedness and ruin, and the other to peace and to God; and we believe that by God's grace we left the first, where we had been securely walking, and took the last. And it now seems strange to us that we ever walked there. Our standards of what is right and wise, of what is true and pure, have so changed. It is difficult to think of Martin Luther, for example, as punished by his parents in his boyhood for stealing cherries and nuts, and the thousand petty offenses which little hands are tempted to commit; the same Martin Luther whose great name the world now honors. It is difficult for you and me to review our past lives, especially during the period of our youthful indiscretions, errors and sins, and realize that we are the same as when we wandered in those devious paths. But just as amid the flux of matter, from childhood to manhood, we have the same bodies; so, notwithstanding these great moral revolutions which come through the power of truth, we have the same moral identity; as the outer man is the same, so is the inner man.

The text reads : " Thou writest bitter things against me, and make me to possess the iniquities of my youth." And the subject which I shall discuss is

THE SENSE OF PROPERTY IN SIN.

I. In the abstract, every man hates sin, and does not like to be held guilty of it; to be regarded having property in it. This proves that his nature comes from God. No man can say anything in favor of the dignity of man's nature, as God made it, and even as in his best moments, every man would himself have it, from which I shall dissent. So far as I know, this is true of all orthodox Christians. The main point of difference between ourselves and those who call themselves liberal Christians is whether in man's present condition he has the power of self-recovery; whether the not-life of his spiritual nature can, without God, produce life. We say the Bible teaches and experience teaches that it cannot. The Apostle Paul puts it just as we find it : " I delight in the law of God, after the inward man; but I see another law in my members, warring against the law of my mind, and bringing me into captivity to the law of sin, which is in my members." You cannot say anything in praise of goodness in the abstract, which men will not approve. This is one of the troubles with those who preach liberal doctrines, so-called. They fall into this agreeable way of dealing with the evil which is in the world; presenting aspects of truth to which men universally give assent, and giving them credit, for being

as good as their own ideal standards; dwelling upon that
in man, which delights in the law of God, and not upon
that other law in our members; which wars against it,
and which needs to be broken up.

Now, no man is always, or even usually as good as his
own ideal standard. The text reads: " Thou writest
bitter things against me." Men write bitter things against
themselves. Take the thoughts of men, as they lie
awake in the night-watches, when they are sick, or when
some great trouble makes them wakeful; they have not
an enemy in the world who is so severe on them as they
are sometimes on themselves. In the Psalmist's phrase:
" They break all their own bones ! " We have a proverb
that listeners seldom hear any good of themselves. Let
a man listen to the voice of his own conscience as he
lies there, all the rest of the world asleep; isolated to
himself; and thinks over his weaknesses, and blunders
and sins. He hears no good of himself. These things
would not be especially bitter unless they were true.
False accusations he can endure; the testimony of
people who do not care for the truth; to whom a false-
hood that is plausible comes as a godsend ; whose tongue
has under it the poison of asps. But, as he lies there
alone, he possesses his iniquities only to condemn them ;
and despise himself so for them.

Look at this fact; that we condemn things in others
which in ourselves we allow; just the opposite to what
it ought to be. A man ought to love his own purity
and honesty and honor better than that of anybody else.

A man's conscience was intended to be his own friend, and not another man's enemy. If he is seeking to be perfect, to be like Jesus of Nazareth, it will be so. In the Sermon on the Mount, the Great Teacher said: "And why beholdest thou the mote that is in thy brother's eye, but considerest not the beam that is in thine own eye?" The conscience is the organ of moral vision. It is the man, with a beam in his own eye, who is most active in looking after the mote in his brother's eye; his beam makes him so uncomfortable, and he would fain persuade himself that it is his brother's mote. The most self-indulgent men are the severest in their judgment of other men. The man who wants the most rigidly to press home the dictate of his conscience upon you; to prescribe the rule of life which you ought to adopt; get at his manner of living, as between himself and his conscience, and in nine cases in ten you will find that it is self-indulgent; he is exercising the strength of his moral nature on the lives of other people. I was dining with a man in another city who, as was his usual custom, had his wines on the table; and, without being rallied on the subject, he entered at once upon the defense of the practice; and one of his arguments was that none of the professed teetotalers were absolutely so; did not sometimes indulge in the use of stimulants. I told him that was not the result of my observation of them; though perhaps there were notable instances where it was true. But, doubtless, the principle of his remark, he found right here: When men press home too rigidly, their ideas of what other men ought to do, they are tempted to be lax in their own practices ; and, perhaps, in the very direction of his rigidity. The principle is a sound one.

This is true, that while men do not see themselves as others see them, they likewise do not see themselves as they see others. They do not apply that moral standard, which God has given them, so that they can walk uprightly, and, therefore, securely, to themselves, as they apply it to other men. If you and I were as good Christians as other people ; would they accept our standards for them ; would be sure to become, we should be very different from what we are ; we should pray more, we should study the Bible more, we should sin less. All this shows us that we have a law in our minds which is hostile to evil; that whatever our practice, our ideal is right; accords with that of the Bible, and of God Himself. Therefore, it is that we do not like to confess that any sin is our own ; that we have property in it, and that when a sin is brought home to our door we do just as Adam did, when he said to God's inquiry after his conduct in reference to the forbidden fruit : " The woman whom Thou gavest to be with me, she gave me of the tree, and I did it eat ;" and as Eve did, " The serpent beguiled me and I did eat." We try to transfer it as property to another.

II. Property in sin cannot be shifted, like other property, from man to man.

In law, that is, in law's theory, there is nothing

more sacred than the right of property, and yet there is nothing that is more easily passed from hand to hand. What is yours to-day is another man's to-morrow. This transfer of property from one man to another, this interchange of our property in money for a commodity, or something which is convenient or comfortable for us, is the very foundation of all trade, national or international. The railroads, the ships of the ocean are only bearing back and forth the property which is changing hands. The pulsations of national and international life are transmitted along the channels of trade: rivers, canals, railroads, the oceans. And yet, in a stricter sense, there is almost nothing we can call our own. As having a life-tenure upon this planet, we call ours, what we can control the use of while we live: the houses we put up, the land we purchase and fence in, the books we write and publish. But the Bible teaches us that we can carry nothing away with us. These city improvements, which occupy so much of our time, the lots we purchase and grade, the buildings we plan and erect; yes, they are ours, in a sense. That is, we have paid money for them, we have deeds of them, but who will hold the deeds to-morrow? who can tell? Somebody; God only knows who.

The only thing we have to hold and carry away with us is character; is what we are in the hidden man of the heart; so what we have is not ours, only what we are. When an evil deed is committed in a city the first question is: " Whose property is that deed?" The man who did it owns it. It belongs to no one else in all the

universe. And the great effort of the author of that
deed and of those who try to defend him, is to show
that he had no property in it; that he was not there in
person to do it; that if he did it, he did it without mali-
cious intent. It is true that he is not the only one who
has personal interest in what he has done. It often hap-
pens that the wrong-doer is almost the last one to realize
the nature and magnitude of his crime; that he bears
lightly what falls with crushing weight upon his parents,
his family; that he is so bent upon escaping the penalty
of it, that he regards the effort of civil authority to ar-
rest and punish him an extraordinary warfare upon his
person.

A man gets property in sin, just as he gets it anything
else: by making an outlay of himself to secure or accomplish it. Evil cannot be bought and sold for money.
The only way a man can ever get property in sin, is by
selling himself. It is true that in the last analysis a man's
honestly earned money; that which he has got by the
sweat of his brow, is himself. This is why it is called
his, because he has put so much of himself into it. So
that the evil which he gives his money to accomplish,
even though accomplished by the hand of another, is so
far forth his property. Neither can a man get rid of his
property in sin by paying money. In these days, in
some of our cities, at least, it is supposed to be within the
limits of possibility to buy out the law. Corrupt men
know how to manipulate juries, so that the ends of human justice are defeated, and the guilty go free. The

recent uprising in a city of the interior, was intended to be a protest against this method of relieving men whose hands were blood-red with murder from their property in evil. Thirty or forty lives were sacrificed, and a great city was thrown into a riot, because the people believed the law to be so administered that men who had property in sin were relieved of it.

As between man and man there is no equivalent, there is no consideration, on account of which property in sin can be transferred. He who commits sin enters into a transaction which is not strictly and primarily between man and man; between himself and another man. It is between himself and God. Can a man who, by putting an obstruction on a railroad track, hurls a number of his fellow-beings to instant death, cripples and defaces for life a number more; interrupts traffic and travel for hours; can this man settle up with the railroad company or with the survivors or the relatives of the dead? It is true that a man can often do something to mitigate the sufferings of others from his wrong-doing. But this does not relieve him of his property in this act. It is true that wrong-doing often enters into God's plan as a source of benefit to those not injured by it; neither does this relieve him of such property.

You remember in Dickens' "Our Mutual Friend," how Bradley Headstone, who though he had taken the life of another man, tried to shift his property in the deed upon Roger Riderhood, by copying his clothes, and his neckties; by shaking blood upon him as he lay

asleep ; and yet, when he went back to his school, how
his deed haunted him ; deprived him of his sleep ; made
him cower before the innocent faces of his pupils ; and
when Roger Riderhood appeared in his school, with the
bundle of clothes in which the foul deed had been done,
how he trembled before him.   And you remember how,
the next day, being Saturday and a holiday, though
Bradley Headstone was to have no more holidays, how
in order to be rid of this man Riderhood, who threat-
ened to live with him, to eat and sleep with him, till he
had given him the last penny he earned ; Bradley Headstone, with this shadow of his evil deed beside him, walked
on the banks of the canal ; you remember the death-grap-
ple between them, and how they both went into the
watery depths, and their bodies were found there under
the ooze and scum, still in that last struggle.   The property in sin had not been shifted ; it had been taken by
the owner elsewhere !

The sense of property in sin, because we have in-
vested our wills in it, that it is a man's own possession ;
being followed by it as by a shadow ; being haunted by
it as by the presence of something we loathe ; condemn-
ing ourselves for it ; for the folly of it, the ignominy of
it, the madness of it ; the consciousness that our own
estimate of it is just what would be the estimate of every
living being in the universe, could he be made acquainted with it ; the feeling that God knows it and
condemns it ; that He keeps His omniscient eye on it,
day and night, as our property, saying to us, through our

conscience, and by His speech : " Thou art the man ! '"
and that at length, when men are judged for deeds
done here in the body, we must stand before His bar and'
give account of it ; this must make existence a burden
to a sinner wherever he may be !

Take this experience of Job ; what was the occasion
of it ? It was simply God's letting him come into possession of his own, making him heir to his own youth !'
Job does not complain of it as unjust. God had been
dealing with him so that all his past, and especially the
past of his youth, when his blood was hot, when his will
was strong, and when his judgment was imperfect and he
did not know it, came back as his own. God showed'
him his title-deed to those iniquities. The great plea
which men urge, when told of a judgment-day and the
penalties of another life, is that all they want is to be
treated according to their deserts. This is precisely
what awaits us all : judgment according to the deeds of
the body ; judgment according as every man's work
shall be. And this is precisely where Job felt the press-
ure of God's hands. " Thou writest bitter things against
me, and makest me to possess the iniquities of my youth."
There is no danger that the Judge of all the earth will
be confused as to a man's identity ; as to his where-
abouts ; as to his agency in sin ; as to his property in it.
Peter never will be accused of betraying Christ, nor
John of denying Him with an oath. But every man
will possess his own sin, and not another man's.

If these positions are correct, namely, first, that every

man instinctively hates sin as property belonging to himself, and does not like to be charged with it as his property, to be held guilty of it and accountable for its consequences ; and if again property in sin cannot be shifted
from man to man, cannot be converted into freedom
from sin ; what is the condition in which we who have
been sinning all our lives long ; who have to answer for
sins of childhood and sins of youth ; sins of manhood
and womanhood ; sins of middle life and sins of old age ;
wat is the condition in which we find ourselves ? This
question prepares us for some of the strong expressions
of Revelation respecting what God in Jesus Christ has
done to transfer sin, to take away sin. And I remark :

III. God has provided a way by which sin as our personal property, sin as our possession, can be disposed of.
This is the great fact of the Bible. The great fact out
of the Bible is sin : sin as man's work, sin as man's
memory, sin as man's degradation, sin as the source of
man's apprehension. The great fact in the Bible is
God's method by which a man can put away sin ; his
own sin ; so that it shall never more be his possession, so
that he shall lose the very sense of property in it.

There can be no way of putting away a man's
sins ; of transferring them, of getting rid of them,
without God is a party to it. God has purposely made
us so, that, in our best moods, we think about sin,
just as He does ; in our secret souls we think so about
our own sins. And, what we term conviction of sin
is God's Spirit letting His light in upon our sins,

emphasizing them in such a way that we see that they are still written against us; that though not recalled by us for years, they are there; and though memory has not brought them back as ours, they still are ours. This is a world full of sinful people. The majority, probably the large majority of people in any city, or community at any one time, would, in candor, acknowledge that they are not living according to the dictates of their own consciences; that they are allowing in themselves things which they condemn in others; things which belittle them in their own eyes; and which, if disclosed, would belittle them in the eyes of other men, who are sinful like themselves. And yet God has so set men together in family, civil and social relations; so bound them together by ties of intercommunication, and interdependence, that a man can seldom commit flagrant sins in his youth without their following him all his days.

In September, 1850, while Mr. Webster was still Secretary of State, he gave a dinner to the alumni of Dartmouth College, of whom he himself was one; *primus inter pares.* During the dinner, some one said to Mr. Webster, of his argument in the Girard Will case: "That was the greatest effort in your life!" Mr. Webster playfully said, he believed that remark had been made of all his efforts; and so he proposed, in his familiar way, to pass the question round to the guests present, as to which one was really entitled to be called his greatest effort. Among those mentioned by the guests were, " The Eulogy

on Adams and Jefferson," "The Reply to Hayne,"
"The Address at Bunker's Hill," "The Eulogy of the
Pilgrims at Plymouth Rock," "The Greek Revolution,"
and "The Panama Mission." The question then came
back to Mr. Webster himself. He replied, by subordi-
nating all his other great efforts to his plea before the
Supreme Court for his Alma Mater. "How came I to
be retained in the Girard Will case? How came I to
be sent to Congress from Massachusetts so soon after
removing there? How came I to have laid before me
the occasion of the efforts you have honored by your
encomiums? How came I to be so highly appreciated
in Great Britain? It was all, primarily, owing to the
reputation, which, when feeling that my Alma Mater was
being deeply wronged, I won in my effort to defend her."

That act was Mr. Webster's personal property, as all
our noble acts are ; as all our sinful acts are. It brought
him no large fee. In it he stood against his native State,
and against her Supreme Court. He was then in his
thirty-seventh year. When he was sixty-nine he delib-
erately gave it as his opinion that that act done in his
thirty-seventh year, did more to determine and control his professional and public career than any other
act of his life. No man ever knows what act of his will
most determine his moral destiny. It is coming in somewhere. Oftentimes it is one of those acts of which the
patriarch speaks : a deed of our youth ! That deed is
like one of many crowns afterwards to be won ; it is
like a millstone hung around his neck. If he would for-

get it, the world will not let him; if he would outlive
it, some gray-haired veteran still lingers somewhere on
earth to tell the tale. This illustrates just how in nature,
as we say ; under His providential economy, God has
fixed it so that a man shall possess his own deeds, good
or evil.

2. There can be no method of putting away a man's
sins without he himself is party to it and pacified by it.
In this respect sin is like all other property. It
cannot be parted from us but by our consent. And
here is where I would put emphasis upon man's
dignity. " In the image of God made He them !" It
is man's glory to be made like God, in that which is
God's highest glory: namely, in his moral nature. It is
not God's highest glory that He made the heavens and
the earth, that by Him all things consist. It is not
man's highest glory that he cultivates the earth and sub-
dues it; that he clothes it with harvests and flocks ; that
he gives his merchandise the wings of steam ; and flashes
his words along the pathways of the lightning. Man's
highest glory is that he may be one with God, by be-
coming like Him. What God approves in man, that
only in his inmost soul he must approve in himself. He
does not approve in himself the unrest of his nature ;
the spiritual ennui and discontent which often cloud his
horizon ; nor of the sin out of which these spring. The
language of his spirit is, and it goes up in secret places
to the ear of God : " Oh ! wretched man that I am, who
shall deliver me from the body of this death?"

You say it is an easy matter for God to forgive sin. He has only to exercise the infinite grace of His nature and the deed is done. But forgiveness is like any other gift. It requires the participation of two persons. It requires one to forgive and the other to be forgiven. It requires one to give the gift of grace and another to take it. This property, which you and I have in sin, has to be transferred, or it will remain ours forever. "On Him was laid the iniquity of us all!" Do we say so? The property, which God has in grace, has to be transferred or it is His forever. " I am He that blotteth out thy transgressions for My own sake." Forgiveness is with God; but the consent to forgiveness, the agreement to be reconciled to God as one, who has forgiven for His own sake; that is with man, that is with you and me.

You have seen a little child, whose mother has crossed his will, has denied him something, reproved him for something wrong, hang aloof from her kisses, turn his face away from her smiles, refuse to be reconciled on the basis of this limitation. This very nature is in you and me with reference to God's forgiveness. It is not irreverent to say that there is no forgiveness in God; I mean the depths of His love have no resources of forgiveness; His infinite grace has no expedients of forgiveness that can reach one who does not yearn to be forgiven. This is where men make the great mistake of life with regard to this subject. It seems to them that if God has such tenderness and patience; that if He is

not willing that any should perish, but that all should
come to repentance ; why the obligation under which
they put Him whenever they conclude to give over trans-
gression is so great, that they have nothing to fear. They
have this to fear : That they may be so confirmed in a
disposition to live in a world that God has made ; to
breathe the air which He has so wondrously adapted to
their lungs ; to become familiar with His ten thousand
voices of warning, persuasion, entreaty, while they allow
them to pass by as the idle wind, and yet not be forgiven ; that it will abide with them forever ! So far as
the Bible goes we know of nothing more that God proposes to do. So far as our conjecture or imagination
can go we know nothing more that God can do. Now,
what do you and I propose to do ?

3. There can be no method of putting away a man's
sins without God and man are both party to it. Property has to be transferred by people who consent together to the transfer. It is so of this property. It is
a transaction which requires not only the action of two
separate individualities, but their concurrent action !
Such action is possible ; such action is provided for by
God Himself with reference to sin. I have tried in this
discourse to make emphatic the sense of property in sin,
the truth that it is not something of a general nature ;
like the air or the light which we breathe ; in which we
see ; and thus make them ours, but something which belongs to each man and to no one else, because he creates
it ; his personality goes into it. I think this truth com-

mends itself to every man's conscience in the sight of God. The Bible calls us sinners because we make sin, just as a man is called a hatter because he makes hats. Now, with this impression fresh in memory, I want to cite to you some of the representations of the Bible. For example, take the words of John the Baptist to his disciples : "Behold the Lamb of God that taketh away the sins of the world." To the Hebrew mind that implied a transfer; a victim at the altar of sacrifice surrendering His life as a propitiation for sin ; standing in the place of the sinner as a sinner, that the sinner might be released. Take again the words of the Apostle Paul in the 2d Epistle to the Corinthians : "For God hath made Him to be sin for us who knew no sin, that we might be made the righteousness of God in Him." Here is a method by which the sinner's property in sin may be transferred to One who has no property in sin ; in which, at the same time, God's property in righteousness may be transferred to one who has no righteousness. You say you do not understand it. I do not ask you to understand it. God does not ask you to understand it. You who are not learned in the law will stand in the presence of your advocate, your counselor, and set your seal to a document you never wrote, couched in language the very phraseology of which is obsolete ; language the meaning of which is cumbered by hundreds of legal glosses and interpretations ; and because your legal adviser says, write your name there, you do it without a misgiving. I bring you this document of your

Father's love, written by His hand and sealed with His
name in the blood of His Son ; and I assure you that if
you will put your soul's-signature there, your property in
sin shall be transferred to that Mighty One on whom God
has laid your help ; and His property in righteousness
shall be transferred to you, so that it shall seem to your
soul as though His own lips repeated the words : " De-
part in peace, thy sins are forgiven thee !"   And what
is your answer ?   Will you be justified by faith and have
peace with God through the Lord Jesus Christ ?   Will
you let the love of God break down the wall of partition
between Him and yourself ?   Will you accept what God
proposes ? Will you take His Son Jesus Christ, the Lord,
as your mediator between Himself and yourself ?   Will
you pass your property in sin over upon Him who knew
no sin, that He may take it away ?

> Lo the Lamb of God, my soul!
>   Patient here thy nature wearing,
> Wounded sore, to make thee whole,
>   All life's burdens with thee sharing;
>   Numbered with transgressors He,
>   Bearing thine iniquity !
>
> By one man came death through sin ;
>   Vain our sorrow and contrition ;
> By One Man comes peace within ;
>   By One Man comes full remission.
>   Bruised reed, He will not break,
>   He forgives for His own sake !

Tempted like as thou art here,
  Formed, O wonder! in thy fashion,
Sharing human joy and tear,
    Full of grace and sweet compassion;
      Lo the Lamb of God, to-day!
      He will take thy sin away!

Reach thy finger! Lo his hands!
  To the cross for thee they nailed Him,
Stood around in mocking bands,
    With their taunts and jeers assailed Him.
      Left of God in agony,
      Ah! my soul, it was for thee.

Reach thy hand! behold His side!
  Be not faithless, but believing,
In that cleft for sinners hide,
    Cleansing, healing, there receiving.
      Lo! my soul, the Lamb of God!
      He for thee death's pathway trod.

CPSIA information can be obtained
at www.ICGtesting.com
Printed in the USA
BVHW04*1044170918
527708BV00015B/1845/P